# God's Resume

## A Collection of Spiritual Poems

Ronnie Fletcher

 www.trafford.com

North America & international
toll-free: 1 888 232 4444 (USA & Canada)
fax: 812 355 4082

## <u>Acknowledgements</u>

I would like to thank Bishop T.D. Jakes of the Potters House, Bishop Carlton Brown of Bethel Gospel Assembly of Harlem, NYC and Pastor Joel Olsteen of Houston Texas for sharing their spiritual and motivational sermons. Listening to some of these sermons has inspired me to write a number of the works which are included in this book of poems. I pray that you enjoy reading these poems and can find comfort from them.


Ronnie Fletcher

# Table of Contents

# God's Resume

Have you ever sat down to think of what He has done?

If we paid attention, we'd have to admit we're the selfish ones

Let's go down memory lane of the troubles of your past

How you would begin to panic, thinking your life wouldn't last

Or those nights when you felt sick as all hell

Who did you call on, when all you could do is yell?

What about those times that Con Ed threatened to kill your lights?

Who stepped in and told Con Ed not tonight?

Or when you fell on hard times, with nothing to eat

Who lifted your hunger, and placed you back on your feet?

Or when that certain love of your life who deeply hurt you

Whose shoulder was there to catch your tears and see you through?

No matter the problem, no matter your sorrow

He only asked for your faith, as He blessed your tomorrow

Yet all that He's done, while we ignored all His laws

He gave His only son, despite all our flaws

So if you still don't think He deserves your praise today

Like anyone applying for a job, review God's resume

Ronnie Fletcher

4/21/13

1

## A Certified Check

The Lord wrote a check for you and for me

It was drawn by heaven, certified by Thee

When He gave you His spirit, He gave you His trust

So why, when He asks for our faith, do we give such a fuss?

People show lack of faith, yet He still blessed us all

Yet only when we need, is when His name is truly called

Now, from birth, we were certified like a check in hand

Only we listen to each other, something I'll never understand

We always take notice of those who stand out loud

As we watch, with criticism, they seem to be proud

Now when we learn to know the Lord, we feel Him inside

Those who walk tall, with a gleam they cannot hide

As we notice those people, that take pride in their walk

If you ask them how they feel, it's their smile that will talk

With their shoulders up straight and their chest stuck out

You ask how I can learn to have that pride that you shout

That stranger will tell you why his life is not a wreck

It's because the Lord gave his life a certified check

Fletch

3/11/12

2

## Breathe On Us

Today we visited the house of trust
We sang and prayed for the Lord to breathe on us
The Spirit was present in the church today
While we sang out loud, we continued to pray
When the Spirit flowed, there was little fuss
As we continued to ask the Lord to breathe on us
Now don't get me wrong, we had to conceive
As people gave praise, people began to believe
Some felt the Spirit lift their fears
While others sat and wondered why their eyes grew tears
But while all this happened, nobody could fuss
As the house asked the Lord to breathe on us
We asked Him to relieve all of our pains
Breathe your blessings as we feel your rain
We asked Him to chase whatever was wrong
The Spirit continued to show its presence was so strong
So Lord, thank you, because your blessings are a must
As we pray for you to breathe on us

Fletch
6/12/11

# THE DEAL

AS I SAT IN CHURCH PONDERING WHAT IS REAL

THE BISHOP SPOKE OUT ABOUT COMPLETING THE DEAL

HE SPOKE OF HOW PEOPLE COME TO CHURCH TO ASK FOR GOD'S GRACE

YET THE LIFE THEY LIVE, SHOWS THEY LIE TO GODS FACE.

WHY DO SOME PEOPLE COME TO SING AND GIVE HIM PRAISE?

WHEN THEY CAN ONLY RETURN TO THEIR OWN WICKED WAYS

YOU CAN WALK THE WALK; YOU CAN SMILE LIKE YOU CARE

WHO DO YOU THINK YOU'RE FOOLING, AS THE LORD PULLED UP A CHAIR

NOW YOU CAME TO MY HOUSE TO GIVE YOUR LIFE TO ME;

HAVE YOU FORGOTTEN YOUR PROMISE?  I'M THE ONE KNOWN AS THEE

WHEN YOU GAVE YOURSELF TO ME, YOU SAID YOU WERE FOR REAL

SO HOW WOULD YOU BE IF I DIDN'T KEEP MY PART OF THE DEAL?

DID YOU WAKE UP THIS MORNING?  DID YOU SEE THE DAYLIGHT?

IMAGINE HOW YOU'D BE IF YOU ROSE WITHOUT YOUR SIGHT

YOU WOULD QUESTION ME. YOU'D TELL ME THEN HOW YOU FEEL.

AND IF I BECAME LIKE YOU

## *WOULD YOU LIKE THE DEAL?*

Fletch

10/23/11

# Love Them Unconditionally

Today we woke up without being judged by Thee

What the Lord asked of us, is that we love unconditionally

You will cross the path of a different person every day

Don't be a judge of that stranger, they might've had a troubled way

As we walk through life, we feel driven by a force

Yet he walks by our side to keep us on course

The spirit of our Lord dwells from within our heart

Yet all He requires is that we all do our part!

Have you ever given a true look at the symbol of Christ?

It's a man standing tall with his arms extended in sacrifice

We all are presents wrapped up by the touch of Thee

As we smile with His chill, we ask why did He choose me?

Lord, we are created by you to live and find your path

For those who don't understand, let them do the math

So, if you believe that He died for our sins

Then you will feel His angels, as they guide your winds

And tonight before you go to sleep, remember the words of Thee

Don't judge My presents, just love them unconditionally

Fletch 10/30/11

# A Simple Thing

Now pull up a chair and please sit down

The message I reveal will be the best in town

It's short, but special, so you really need to hear it

As God's voice spoke through the Holy Spirit

Now, each person has no problem complaining to me

But do they give thanks to the one known as Thee?

And it is even easier for all to judge one another

Yet how many are willing to reach out to their brother?

Each morning you awake, I blessed you on that day

Yet you go about your business forgetting to pray

I only ask that you give praise for a minute

Now who claims they're too busy, no time to hear it?

"Oh God" is what I hear when you have a reaction

Whether it's good or bad, now who's a distraction?

I have a simple task for all to try

The next time you have a problem and look to the sky

Take both your hands with your palms facing the sky

Then connect your thumbs and raise them very high

Now you will see a person go from asking of Me

To a grateful person giving their praise to Thee

Your hands went from always seeking new things

To your fingers showing you my angel's wings

Now, how hard was this for you to try?

As I sit here in heaven watching you from the sky

Fletch

11/14/11

## The Devil's Task

Now people have you heard of the evil one?

Promises are made to give riches and fun

So you've been saved and you think you're protected?

The devil can still have you, if his way is selected

He listens to your thoughts; he feeds on your sorrow

When he promises you relief, it is to capture your tomorrow

The people in the Bible all had their weak ways

Yet when they felt God's hand, their nights turned to days

We all live a life that includes some fear

But if we have faith, it's the Lord we will hear

Your walk with the Lord will be simple, if you listen

As we feel the Holy Spirit, The devil will question you, the Christian

Now the devil can only try, if we allow his way in

It's God's hand that will lead you like a true friend

So when you have fears, it's the Lord you should ask

The devil seeks your weakness, that's his task

# Who You Gonna Blame?

Last night I was told to take a close look

Instead of a magazine or paper, read the Good Book

When I gave the excuse that it's truly hard to understand

The statement was asked, "Are you a real man?"

So a challenge of me was now set in motion

She said with knowledge comes strength, and with belief comes devotion

When I stated "I want news, I want to read of others"

She said then you should read the Good Book, it talks of sisters and brothers

The Bible is like a recipe with special ingredients, like spices and herbs

You should start your journey, and read the section called Proverbs

This is a section that will bring you a great surprise

It is a book of knowledge which will truly open your eyes

As I learned to understand the true meaning of right and wrong

The book spoke to me, as it made my spirit grow strong

For you to read the Bible, it will take a lot of your time

But as you grow in your understanding, things will be fine

As a child, our sight is blurry and we can't make a decision

The Bible is our pair of glasses, as it corrects our vision

Just read it for 15 minutes a day, and learn how to live

As you open your heart, it will teach you to forgive

But to just let the Good Book sit would be a crying shame

Without reading it to learn, now who's to blame?

Fletch

1/19/12

## Do You Truly Believe

As I woke up this morning with troubles of the heart

I thought to myself, how would my day start?

With my worries in my mind, no answers to retrieve

The question came to my heart, do you truly believe?

Did you know the Devil cannot approach you without God's permission?

That's because God has placed us all on our own separate missions

When the evil spirits rise, as they all seem to hover

It's God's only hand that tells you, I got you covered

We all ask the question, why God, do you forsake little me?

Instead of trusting in the Lord, the one known as Thee

If you have any questions, if you really want the facts

Then please find a bible, and turn to the section called Acts

Do you remember when rent was due, or when you had no lights?

What about your arguments, do you remember those ugly fights?

You got past those things, when there seemed no way out

Was that the only time you felt the Lord deserved a shout?

Learn that God only expects you to do what you can do

Don't worry about another, just worry about you

Just realize that you are only one person, just stop your greed

God doesn't give you what you ask, He gives you what you need

So just stop your worries, you've got to fight, so pull up your sleeves

As the Holy Spirit descends, the only question is, "Do you truly believe?"

Fletch

2/5/12

9

## The Story of Gwen

Now tonight was a night I listen to a friend

A precious lady who goes by the name of Gwen

She called to my attention of her troubled past

How she lived in the moments, how her riches died so fast

Married with children, she felt she had it all

Until God stripped her of her possessions, and allowed her to fall

She seemed to be lost, without losing her belief

God, please forgive my past, and give me relief

We are talking of a woman who lived a troubled life

While working, she was dealing, she continued as a wife

Until one day, all her troubles seemed so small

This was a day that she received God's true call

Awakened one evening, by the darkness of the night

She was told by the doctors, she would soon lose her sight

Now, Gwen was a strong believer, as she trusted in Thee

She spoke to the Lord, as she asked "How could this be?"

The room was silent, and there remained the darkness of night

Gwen refused to give in, as she heard the Spirit say alright

Doctors came to her on the very next day

Expecting the worst, without knowing what to say

She opened her eyes as she felt God's light

The doctors were stunned to see God gave Gwen sight

You are my miracle from way back when

As she shed tears telling the story of Gwen

Fletch

2/5/12

10

## He Would Love to Hear It

Do you remember how you called to Me?

When you had your problem, you remembered Thee

Last night while you needed someone to blame

You couldn't face a mirror, because it revealed your shame

But when I came as a stranger, I called to you last night

It was you who turned away, thinking I wanted a fight

Why do people think they are better than another?

I gave you different faces, but all are sisters and brothers

What will it take for all to come together as one?

I gave you a world to share, under one heated sun

Do you remember when I sent my Son, Jesus Christ?

Instead of receiving Him, your world made Him a sacrifice

So I ask, what will it take for the world to listen to me?

Since people only call to blame, or cry out "how could this be?"

Life is quite simple, just trust in the Lord, because He is the way

You will receive His blessings on any given day

So when you are ready to be a believer of the Holy Spirit

Give yourself to Jesus! He would love to hear it.

Fletch

5/29/12

# We are Prayin' for You

Today we met a lady who wanted her own child

She and her husband had been trying for quite a while

In her first two attempts her child was stillborn

So on her third attempt, she thought she would have to mourn

But this time, before she had a chance to become so blue

The nurses told her, "Sister, we are all prayin' for you"

She decided this time, instead of her having a sad day

They found the Lord, as they decided to kneel down and pray

She prayed for a healthy baby, and truly nothing more

As the Lord heard her prayers, she delivered a baby to adore

She was puzzled how she contracted this very rare disease

The nurse told her, "Girl you need to pray, and it starts on your knees"

She became pregnant again, but this child had new trouble

But the Lord stepped in, and kept her in His bubble

So today their second child is a healthy little girl

They named her Grace, and welcomed her into this world

Remember we're talking about a couple who started without a clue

Ever since they gave themselves to Jesus, they were shown what to do

So now they tell everyone of their miracle baby story

They've become so grateful, as they give God all the glory

Fletch

6/6/12

12

## From Weakness She GREW Strength

Today we met a lady who spoke of her troubled past

She was a young white lady who was teased while in class

The abuse that she encountered didn't stop when she left school

She spoke of her father who was also very cruel

To hear this woman say she grew up hating white people

Was a shock as we thought this was unbelievable

She stated she met a black girl who welcomed her into her world

A blessing had come to her; it was in the form of this black girl

They did everything together, and for this she was teased by whites

"How could you?" they would say, "Being around them just ain't right"

But her spirit told her to ignore the words of her enemy

Your blessing wears a different color; I gave you eyes to see

She grew up with black people who welcomed her with a smile

As she grew with her only friend, from when she was a child

People will always cross her path as she looks with a smile

As she told her story of her abuse, as a child

The one thing that she learned is that there is good in all

This proud young lady now walks with her head high while standing tall

Fletch

7/30/12

## Be Accountable For Your Ways

Each day something happens we call God's name

When we don't see a solution, there's always someone else to blame

The bible says come to the Lord and sing Him praise

We should acknowledge His blessings and be accountable for our ways

There are moments we feel loss as we always wonder why

These are moments that we raise our heads and search the skies

Now you pray to the Lord when you have a need

The bible says trust in Him, so don't feed your greed

Those who seek His hand give Him all their praise

This will take your heart as you learn to change your ways

How many times has the Lord come through?

Yet all He asks is that praise comes from you

We continue to go through life expecting simple things

It seems like most go through life riding on His angel's wings

The day will come when we shall be accountable for our ways

The question will be asked; why didn't you sing me praise?

Fletch

10/1/12

# Mom's Blessed Oil

Today we met a man who spoke of his healings

He spoke about an accident of his past dealings

Now he spoke about his life as he grew up in sin

His parents had him in church where his heart hadn't been

He was caught in an explosion with no chance to talk

Spoke if 261 surgeries, but he was still able to walk

His face was blown up, he lost his face and body parts

As the doctors challenged if he would live, they said who'd question our smarts?

He spoke of his mom who kept applying blessed oil

Since God had other ideas, as his mom's love couldn't be spoiled

She would come to his side, she put oil where his hand used to be

The doctors couldn't understand how he was blessed by Thee

The same doctors told his mom her son wouldn't speak

As she applied her blessed oil, he was no longer weak

Everything the doctors said he would never do

God took him by the hand, and whispered I got you

He spent several years in hospitals seeking repairs

As God touched his spirit, the doctors could only fear it

Today he tells his story, as his mother enjoys his spirit

If you hear him talk, he now speaks how he feels

He thanks God and his mother, the Holy Spirit is for real

Fletch

10/1/12

15

# Michelle

Today I met a nurse whose name was Michelle

She remembered my story and said I have one to tell

The Lord came to my job to get back my spirit

So please have a seat, here is my story and I would like you to hear it

She spoke of her husband who was very sick for a long time

This was one of the reasons she treated church like a crime

But one day the Lord sent a message through a patient, at her workplace

This lady told her "I pray your soul won't rest until you occupy God's space"

Michelle told her "I pray to the Lord for only three things;

A closer walk, to renew my faith, and to restore my joy before Spring"

What she didn't realize was how awesome God could be

While she prayed for her spirit, the Lord began to set her free

Her husband passed, and for this, He relieved her grief

Sad for her loss, but she began to feel relief

She vowed to find a house of worship, as she continues to pray

As time goes by, she is grateful for every single day

Michelle also asked the Lord to restore her joy

The Lord called on His angels, toward her he would deploy

So now she goes to work with a smile, as she feels the Lord's new touch

Never had she realized how the Lord loved her so much

I felt happy for Michelle, because she is like a child with a toy

As she enjoys her final wish, the Lord restored her joy

Fletch

10/18/12

## From Darkness to His Light

Today I heard a story of a man's troubled past

His demons were within, as his life was fading fast

He practiced black magic, as he learned of evil spells

The Devil had captured his heart, in his living hell

As he lived in darkness, painted on his walls

Covered to the ceiling, as his memory could recall

Robert spoke of his sadness, while he sat with his wife

He thought of wanting to die, ending his sad life

His cousin saved him as he went to leap out the window

This little 4 year old wouldn't allow him to go

So he lay down in his dark room, with a saddened heart

But he didn't realize the Holy Spirit did its part

It was God's hand which saved him from that final leap

As he told his story, his wife began to weep

While he lay down in the room, a light came from Thee

He was puzzled how this light was meant to set him free

While the light shined, he heard songs about the Spirit

He asked other family members, "listen can you hear it?"

They all awoke puzzled, startled by his fright

The Lord had taken Robert from darkness to His light

Fletch

11/14/12

# The Right Destination

Today we listened to the word of the wise

As the preacher spoke, he told all to downsize

Focus on more than your troubles and frustrations

Only God knows your path, only He knows your destination

Some problems seem so heavy, it's like you're in a wrath

It's like driving your car, stay focused on the path

Proverbs 4 tells us to focus our attention

Yet without the wisdom, we lose our connection

Life has its obstacles that cause us all to stray

But the message was on focus, on this new Sunday

So why do we continue to lose focus and live in frustration?

This could be one reason we don't reach our destination

Once you give yourself to Christ, it's then He plants His seed

So you will feel His Spirit, and your mind will begin to feed

The more you seek the word, it's you who'll become wise

As the seed grows, your new world will be a surprise

Those troubles that caused you headaches and frustration

Leave them to Jesus, He has the right destination

Fletch

1/14/13

## Take My Hand

As time is short for all on Earth

We take for granted what life is worth

Each day we awaken is a day we should rejoice

Because one day the Lord may take away that choice

We just expect life to continue with hope for more

Until the unforeseen opens up a darkened door

Some go to church to look for a new day

While others believe in their hearts, but refuse to pray

We never know the path we will take

Until life shows us our next mistake

But if we could just stop and walk the footsteps of another

Then we might see a different life and call all our brothers

You never understand today until you live through tomorrow

Life will bring happiness, but it can also bring you sorrow

But if we all could take a moment to give praise to Thee

Then together we could learn, and "I" could turn to "we"

So let's walk together to face the path of fear

Since without the touch of Thee, none of us would be here!

Fletch

1/14/13

## Life's Change

For us to try a change of life

We must be willing to feel the pain like a knife

For us to become free of the troubles of today

We must first forgive the sins of yesterday

If we review our lives from our past

That's when we will realize we are in God's grasp

The bible says that God is the light

So walk from the darkness and you'll be alright

The skies and the water are clear reflection

It's the Lord's will that gives us direction

The path to the Lord goes through His son

As we pray for forgiveness, we're told of The One

For all to walk in the light of the Lord

It will take life's change for you to applaud

So renew your mind, it will free your spirit

As the Lord's light shines, your skin will feel it

Are you willing to make life's final exchange?

You must first be willing to accept life's change

Fletch

1/22/13

# Renewing Your Mind

The presence of God is a change of living

Are you willing to accept? Do you have the spirit of giving?

Don't try to please your friends and family

God is the light that makes your reality

For those who go to church, that's only the start

Change your mindset, and God will do His part

The bible states that you can have all that you request

Are you willing to change? Are you willing to give your best?

Once you learn to accept God's way to live

Then it will be clear, as you start to forgive

Luke 11-13 states the hunger for God is a love affair

Desire God's presence, show Him how you care

The same way we read the newspaper every day

Replace it with the word, learn how to pray

What about at night, when you crave a snack?

Pick up your bible, and just read one fact

Once you have learned how to replace anger with smiles

Then you will be honored, as you witness God's child

So today you can start by trying to be kind

It will soon be your path to renewing your mind

Fletch

1/22/13

## We Lost a Friend

As winter's breeze cooled the air

It was our Lord's hand who cared

The preacher's voice was deep yet strong

It was the arms of God where we belong

-Let Us Pray-

Now come in people and please sit down

On this sad day, love was found

It takes death of one to make family right

So kneel before me, let's thank God tonight

-Let Us Pray-

Lord we ask you to hear our words

Our hopes are high, just like the birds

We lost a friend so dear to us

Our faith in you is what we trust

-Let Us Pray-

The preacher raised his arms up high

He yelled to all as we began to cry

His words were strong, as he spoke of grief

Our long lost friend has found relief

-So Remember-

His spirit rose to seek the Lord

It rose with faith as we did applaud

The Lord then spoke, remember Thee

I've blessed your friend who is now here with Me

Fletch

1/25/13

## A Look at Life from Thee

Last night while winter's cold came to visit

There was a silent moment, and my mind asked "who is it?"

While all seemed quiet, without any light

The Lord came by to visit me last night

Dreams are windows that we all should not ignore

Like moments in life that come through any door

Treat every moment like you want it to last

Every troubled moment may seem like a task

Come walk with me through the windows of life

With the Lord's embrace, I made no sacrifice

We walked together, His spirit and my soul

As He graced my presence, our story would unfold

We seemed to walk through the sad moments of my past

As time went on, the Lord stated they wouldn't last

As the windows of life allow us to look through

Like a child on Christmas, I was excited by the view

I looked at the story with tears on my face

With the Lord's presence, my past increased its pace

I turned to the Lord to ask Him a question

But before I could speak, a voice drew my attention

The Lord was gone from my side, without a trace

It was His voice from the wind that left tears on my face

The voice of Thee stated I am here when you need

Remember your past and don't get caught up in the greed

Fletch

1/25/13

## What Would You Do?

Now I want to take a moment to give thanks to Thee

Because without all we have, none of us would be

We all go through life wanting for more

Do we ever give thanks for the things we adore?

In Deuteronomy 8.12 it says "eat and you are satisfied"

But do you remember those nights when you sat and cried?

The Lord keeps providing and yet we still don't know how to live

You want to see His glory, then stop taking and learn to give

Selfish people never learn the road to God's way

Because instead of sharing with one another, their focus is led away

They only want to obtain, they only want to receive

Yet they wear a cross, or act like they believe

Now I want you to take a moment to review your past

Every time you had a problem, you thought you wouldn't last

I want you to remember how your troubles seemed so strong

Each time you had to face those demons that did you wrong

Were those the only times you gave your time to pray?

Even when you didn't deserve it, the Lord saved the day

Now we all have these moments when we say this cannot be

Yet the Lord takes our hand, and says now you come with me

So tell me one thing; if our Lord was selfish like you

Without His giving spirit, what would you do?

Fletch

1/30/13

## Yes, I'm to Blame

Everybody has a moment when they need to blame

And to think God almighty would treat us all the same

Yes, He gave us all problems that may seem too hard

While we all complain, it's the bible we disregard

The bible is His message that has the true answers of life

Do we have time to read about the Holy sacrifice?

Now that man is blind, or that lady with the disfigured face

And what about you with your problems and you blame the human race?

I am here to tell you it is all in God's plan

When He is ready, you will feel His holy hand

You see, the only way we respond is when God steps in

We may call it a miracle, as we ask where He's been

Yet what you don't understand, is that God is in control

Only when He is ready, is when the real story will be told

He doesn't mind when we all just whine and complain

Even when we are hurt, we ask Him to take our pain

"Why Lord?" We cry, "Have I felt all this shame?"

Until I touch you my son, yes I'm to blame

Ronnie Fletcher

2/4/13

25

## A Voice

A voice was heard as silence prevailed

It came from those within a jail

But not the jail enclosed with bars

A voice as far away as Mars

Now listen first, before you judge

This voice would move what wouldn't budge

Enjoy your life and think things through

We pay through life for the things we do

So don't think that you'll pass through life

Without your dues paid with a knife

What may seem quick, yet painful too

Is the thing called life, given to me and you

But listen people, for what it's worth

Since when it's gone, you'll share this Earth

A voice can only give you some thoughts

The graves are fenced like old time forts

Since life comes just once in time

Are you ready to lose what's yours and mine?

A voice can only make you aware

It's your decision, so please beware

Since you may not get a second chance

The voice has warned you far in advance

So listen people and stop the crimes

Otherwise your voice will soon join mine

Ronnie Fletcher

2/6/13

## A Birthday to Remember

Today was a day that I had to listen

To a man talk about how he became a Christian

He spoke to me humbled from the very start

Soft spoken yet sincere, as he spoke from the heart

As he spoke to me, he wondered how life could be

I asked his name, and he stated they call me Benzy

When he was a child, only four years old

He was touched by God as his story was told

He was diagnosed with a terminal disease

As his grandmother broke down and begged the Lord, please

Spare his life, and I promise you his spirit

The Lord granted her request, and he is here today to speak it

Benzy talked of how he would try and run from God's hand

Only to be brought back to the Lord's holy land

Each path he would try would seem like a dead end

As he was always led back to his only true friend

After many attempts to find a difficult path

He realized the Lord's power, as he finally did the math

One day a young boy died of cancer at the age of four

And he became a pall bearer, as he received the call

As he walked with the casket held in his hand

The Lord reminded him today is your birthday young man

Ronnie Fletcher

2/6/13

# Are You Their Problem?

Now I want you to review your own child's past

Without you always to their rescue, how long would they last?

Genesis 2:24 says 'teach them and release them'

What once was your blessing is still your heart's gem

How can they learn if you don't let them grow?

And it may be hard, but you must let them go

Some children have problems, they constantly return

But as long as you baby them, how will they learn?

If you want them to be strong, let them face the world

What has now become grown is still your little boy or girl

A tree only grows with very strong roots

This may all seem cruel, but some kids need the boot

They will stumble a bit, and others may fall

But like their first steps, you smiled as they grew tall

The Lord gave you each child for His own purpose in life

Some will become husbands, some will become wives

It is written that the child will mature in their time

But how can this happen if you allow them to whine?

Hard love has its rewards, and this you will see

Set rules for your children, and then set them free

Ronnie Fletcher

2/12/13

# Heavyweight in a Lightweight World

We face a challenge in the world of today

Faced by deceit as our world starts to decay

The Lord shows us signs of how He is in control

Each time a catastrophe happens, a new story unfolds

It's the Lord's fury that we witness in fear

The non believers cry out, because it's the Lord they can't hear

As a heavyweight in this world, you walk strong in God's space

While the lightweights seem lost with fear in their face

A heavyweight is someone well grounded with God's spirit

Sad and confused are the lightweights who can't hear it

While some see your smile even through your pain

Stand up to the world as our God brings His rain

So each time God brings us a Katrina or Sandy

It's to see total strangers come together in a catastrophe

The bible tells us that it's better to give than receive

What God only asks is that we learn to believe

If only people would stop wishing for diamonds and pearls

And just be a heavyweight in a lightweight world


Ronnie Fletcher

3/3/13

## Do You Want the Lord To Do Your Math?

Yesterday I went to McDonalds to get something to eat

A young lady was there hungry by my feet

Now she wasn't asking for a handout or any money

She ordered her own food, a hot tea with some honey

As she searched her suitcase for her change purse

The employees at the store laughed and began to curse

She was embarrassed by their actions and she went away

Still hungry but unable to find her money on this sad day

While she went and sat down with sadness in her eyes

I asked the cashier how much for her food, to his surprise

He told me four dollars or she doesn't get the food

So I said you'd let her starve? Now that's very rude

You work for someone, but that starving person could be you

Give her what she wants, it's God's will you should do

They all stopped and looked at me real strange

When I paid for her meal, I told them keep the change

You never know when the Lord will cross your path

Learn to be humble before the Lord does your math

Ronnie Fletcher

3/5/13

## You're Not By Yourself

As people judge you for no good reason

Do they realize we're all in a special season?

But when God is with you, they can see your wealth

So you should let them know you're not by yourself

When you drive in your car with no one else inside

The Holy Spirit is always along for the ride

There will be times when you will ask God about your health

He will show you signs that you are not by yourself

It is written that we should go by faith and not by sight

And if you truly believe in His word, then you'll be alright

You may not see my Lord, but He is here with me

My God is an awesome God, and my smile is for all to see

So let's bow our heads and give our Lord praise

We should enjoy each moment of our living days

He gives us what we need when He knows it is time

Yet instead of thanking Him, we all decide to whine

Turn to a friend and ask, do you ever remember your hard times?

Yet you're here today, thinking how did I get away with this crime?

When the Devil seeks you out, who can you call without a phone?

The Lord answers all prayers because he never left you alone

Ronnie Fletcher

3/10/13

# God's Still Around

Do you realize that your blessings are your power?

While the Lord blesses you, you grow stronger by the hour

When you cross paths with those non believers

They are helpless as to the Lord's anointed receivers

You don't realize the blessings in your life

Yet the Devil continues to come at you with his knife

If you want the Devil to remain helpless against you

Ignore his words, now this might not be easy to do

Do you realize that if you don't address his negativity

He becomes silent, when he realizes you won't let him be

You will face times when the Devil will invite you to his bed

Offer what you desire to see if your spirit can be fed

But when you cross his path through people of deceit

This will be your moment to see the Lord raise you to your feet

If you want the Devil to stay clear of your path

Just give God your glory, he doesn't want God's wrath

But he will continue to try and break you down

Just smile and let him know God's still around

Ronnie Fletcher

3/14/13

## The Stranger Within Me

Good morning everyone who feels they are in control

Did you hear His voice, as you thought trouble would unfold?

I want you to think about life, when you ask "How could it be?"

We are born with God's spirit; it is the stranger within me

The Lord doesn't look at the shell that everyone else does

Nor does He get alarmed when we say "just because"

While the Lord watches over the path, you question "How could it be?"

Learn to trust the spirit that is the stranger within me

Now, this stranger has always been there, just waiting on you

Allowing life's problems, watching everything that you do

This stranger will let you fall right on your lovely face

But He would never allow you to feel like you've fallen from grace

This stranger you don't know sits on a mighty thrown

Waiting for you to call, without using a telephone

You see, until you accept the Lord, there is a mighty God you shouldn't anger

He will just sit by and continue to act like a stranger

So, give yourself to Christ, and set yourself free

He has always been with you; He's the stranger within me

Ronnie Fletcher

2/25/14

# The Lord Told You

Now I have a question I must ask of you

How long are you going to procrastinate about what you must do?

We all know what road we must take to make things right

So why did you allow yourself to lose sleep last night?

When your landlord gave you those eviction papers, you know why

The Lord told you He would handle it, but you still decided to cry

When the doctor told you it was cancer, without a cure

The Lord told you He would handle it, and with disbelief you questioned "are you sure?"

When your child came to you for clothes or a bite to eat

The Lord told you He would handle it, yet you still show all defeat

The Lord provided the world with a book for all to read

This book is called the Bible, it has the wisdom that we need

The problems that we have, the questions that we ask

This book that we've been given, addresses every task

The Bible speaks of wisdom; it's your path of living worry free

Yet instead of seeking the Lord, you turn your back on Thee

Since wisdom is something that we can surely use

Until you give yourself to Thee, it's His wisdom that you refuse

So, if the Lord tells you that He can handle all

Why do you question Him, if you believe in Him at all?

We are all sinners, yet He still gave us His Grace

It was His son's blood that caused the tears on my face

Fletch

2/20/12

# The Ultimate Gift

Now everyone needs to understand this message of today

This powerful meaning expresses love in a special way

We think love is about sex and our own emotions

Yet would you give up your life without any commotion?

As we look at our Lord's love, it's your spirit He lifts

While Jesus cried out on Calvary, it was the Lord's ultimate gift

Do you really think Jesus was held by nails to that cross?

He was held by His love for us, while experiencing a great loss

Do you think Jesus was crucified on the wood of the cross He created?

His love had no limit for the world that He dated

Until you understand how He so loved the world

You may not realize His devotion to every boy and girl

I want you to think about why so many of your friends are no longer here

Not because you are lucky, not because our Lord doesn't care

Now, if God walked away every time we disappointed His glory

We would all be dead, that would have ended our story

Yet He so loved the world; He suffered the greatest loss

It was His son's love that cried out while nailed to the cross

So before you judge love or refuse a spiritual lift

Remember the true meaning of love, it's the ultimate gift

Ronnie Fletcher

2/23/14

## Lester My Friend

As darkness filled our winter skies
My heart was saddened by my friend's eyes
Sad for a moment, he called in pain
I need your help, as the skies filled with rain
There he was, weak indeed
My friend's heart called, it had a need
Come, my friend, come sit with me
With tears in my heart, I became we
Here was a man who helped everyone in need
Yet when he cried out, all those friends wore greed
I came to his side to help my sick friend
A man I knew from way back when
People lose focus, forget those who cared
When you need a real friend, emptiness is shared
I learned one thing of Lester, my one true friend
His heart was pure, he was a giant among men

Fletch
3/9/04

# How Are You Living?

Today we met a man who spoke of his past

As we listened to his story, his life seemed so fast

He spoke of how he lived without sacrifice

Until he was introduced to the One called Christ

His life consisted of drugs, cars, and a steady cash flow

But what was missing was the family he truly didn't know

While he lived so high with girls and fancy ways

He lived the life of Riley, never counting his days

His drug problem took over his saddened life

He couldn't have done more damage, not even with a knife

Homeless and broke is where his life had turned

Until he met a lady who asked had he learned

She invited him to church, just to hear what it said

Impressed by her beauty, he thought that he was dead

He followed this thing of beauty; he felt what's to lose?

When he arrived at church, it was Christ he had to choose

Each time he entered the church, it erased all his fears

He asked us to forgive him, as his eyes filled with tears

He's a new man today, on his journey with Christ

As he tries to regain what seemed like a sacrifice

So people, we are never too big to be forgiven

It all starts when we change how we are living


Fletch

10/2/11

## Gary's Word

Today was a day we paid God's house a visit

We sat down to listen, as we felt the Holy Spirit

There were ladies in God's house who sang the Lord praise

As they entered the church, each one gave thanks for their days

Strangers were acknowledged in a place they were unknown

While we sat and listened to their songs, our spirits had grown

I watched from the rear as these strangers became friends

So little was required, as they gave praise to no end

"Thank you Lord!" was the cry, as people spoke of their blessings

While others felt their pain, we all got our own lessons

The message was clear as spirits became free

Remember the word and trust in Thee

People don't realize how much energy they waste on hate

Yet they call on the Lord to change their fate

If people would just extend their hand to help one another

Then kindness would return from their sister or brother

When you do kind things for a stranger, by just saying yes

That could be your angel who smiles on your test

So, if you can trust a stranger, or help a friend

Then God will remember your name from way back when

Just reach out to someone, whether it's a woman or man

Offer instead of asking, the kindness of your hand

Fletch

12/18/11

## Hunger For God

We visited a new church in Harlem today

As we listened to the word, it made you want to pray

Pastor Scott delivered a powerful word filled with energy

While I listened to her message, her spirit moved me

The pastor spoke of how we need to be hungry for the Lord

As Pastor Scott spoke, her followers began to applaud

The pastor stated when you are hungry for something, you'll do anything

Yet there are those who think worship is only a fling

When you do things for self pleasure or self gain

This isn't the Lord's way to remove someone's pain

We must learn to hunger and be a servant for the Lord

Do unto others, and help those who can't afford

As we read God's word, it shows we hunger for His way

The Bible has your answers; Are you ready to pray?

You are supposed to do for others, as you feel it in your heart

The reward is serving Jesus, knowing you've done your part

As we go through life, you'll find non-believers without a clue

Yet helping someone without expecting is God's spirit inside of you

So, honor our God and His spirit will cause you to glow

Seek out His word and knowledge, and your spirit will flow

You will become humbled by the spirit, as you find your way

And to think it all started when you knelt down to pray

Ronnie Fletcher

3/17/13

# Your King Is Coming

Now I want you to think about how you are living

Are you following the scriptures, are you someone who is giving?

I want you to look around to see the company you keep

Are they Christians who believe or people who give you the creeps?

Because your King is coming, and with Him comes His glory

Are you one who believes, then get ready for the real story

Now I want you to really ponder whether you'll be around

Because like any King, you will know when He hits this town

Are you willing to confront the Devil and tell him he's a liar?

Can you walk away from sin and throw her to our Lord's fire?

Because the King is coming and His glory is a mighty one

But you must be willing to acknowledge He has the Devil on the run

Now we've heard the whispers of our savior coming to town

I'm here to tell you that our King wears a mighty crown

You must believe that He will bring glory when He arrives

As He listens to His believers, he will humble their troubled lives

All you've been through is because He knows what you bring

No matter how hard it's been, remain loyal to our King

Ronnie Fletcher

4/2/13

## How Dare You

The Lord promised that He would provide

Yet there are those who'd rather run and hide

How can people expect the Lord to give to those sinners?

When He asks only of your belief in Him, as new beginners

Many people say they know the Lord, yet they don't pray

Who are they fooling by acting like a sinner every day?

Many people say they refuse to accept what the Devil gives

Yet as they go through life, they show they don't know how to live

Stop walking around acting like you haven't got a clue

He promised you all you need, so why do you still refuse to?

Give the Lord your praise and watch what He can do

After all He has given, my question is How dare you?

Just humble yourself and don't live on foolish pride

As the Lord listens to your heart, He feels what's inside

But if you continue to live like you haven't got a clue

As you live in sin, my response is How dare you!

Ronnie Fletcher

4/2/13

## God Waited For Me

Today we listened as the Lord's hand was talked about

As we listened to this stranger, the people began to scream and shout

While he spoke about his life as a hardened gangster

This was back in the day when his life wasn't a blur

As he entered the emergency room after being shot in his spine

His family was in a panic as they all began to whine

The nurse informed him that his injury wouldn't allow him to walk

As he laid there heavily medicated, he was unable to talk

When the hospital preacher came to pray over him that day

Barely alive, he gave himself to God, as he himself began to pray

Remember that the nurse informed the family that he wouldn't walk again

As he laid there paralyzed, crying with family and friends

Once he gave his spirit, he suddenly felt a change

He tried to elevate himself, as his eyes saw something strange

While he looked at the preacher praying over him

That's when he saw Jesus' extended hand's reaching out to him

As the nurses began to panic, looking in disbelief

They saw this paralyzed man raise up in his relief

The stranger rose to his feet so he could embrace Christ

While all stood by stunned at the man's great sacrifice

He stated he heard the Lord say "I've waited for you"

Stunned that he could rise, after being told what he couldn't do

But Jesus told him I have waited for you all these years

He responded "Lord I'm sorry" as his eyes filled with tears

Jesus told him you will walk as I've given you a new glory

I've forgiven your past, now go tell all your story

Ronnie Fletcher

4/7/13

42

## Because He Blessed You

There are times in our lives when we forget our path

Many get real comfortable and refuse to do the math

Do you remember the days when you prayed for a chance?

Asked God for His blessings; asked Him to show you how to dance

Do you remember the days when you asked for God's hand?

Didn't know where the rent was coming from, in this distant land

Do you remember how humble you were and only prayed to our Lord?

Now you've become too large in life, a move you cannot afford

Because when you were blessed, you did not appreciate Him

Now you've lost your way, because you went out on a limb

Because when He asked you to do His will and remain humble

You decided you were too good for Him, and this caused you to stumble

Now when you asked God for a job, and He blessed you with one

Because you've been blessed, you're feeling your job is done

Now the Lord sees you cannot handle His blessing without a price

So He reaches down and makes you His next sacrifice

Because when you were humble, God blessed you

Now you needed a reminder of what you need to do

So take heed of the Lord's blessings, because they can be taken away

Now do you understand why you'd better give thanks today?

Ronnie Fletcher

4/16/13

## So You Think I'm Crazy

Have you ever done things that may look crazy to others?

You had no control as you tried to explain to your sisters and brothers

When the Lord gives you the spirit for you to do His work

You may seem crazy to some, while others might call you a jerk

People observe what they don't understand, yet they still want to judge

So when they are called upon, by the spirit, they refuse to budge

It's a sensation that makes you feel like you can't be stopped

That's the Holy Spirit giving you the will that can't be topped

Don't try to explain this to those who judge with the naked eye

As those others ask you questions, just point to the sky

You must understand that people will always judge you by what they see

Yet do they understand the Holy Spirit's power from Thee?

When you are touched by the spirit, your life is out of your control

Feeling God's touch gives you a new view of what will unfold

So don't be ashamed because it's not for you to explain

Just go with the spirit, even if it may seem insane

While there may be times that people may think you've lost your mind

As you look to see who remains, the true Christians will be hard to find

Remember the Lord looks for those who truly believe

Not the wanna bees with something up their sleeve

Ronnie Fletcher

4/19/13

## How Long

Hello you, yes I am talking to you

The one being used, the one who doesn't have a clue

Now this might seem harsh, it might even seem bold

But how long are you going to allow others to be so cold?

Do you have someone who always needs a helping hand?

Never giving of themselves, yet they know you'll understand

Now the Lord didn't put you here to accept someone's abuse

Yet you allow a loved one to always have an excuse

The best thing you can do is allow them to fall

Every time they have a problem, you answer the call

Well, if you really want to help them get back onto their feet

Deny your support and see if it's your smile they greet

There is nothing wrong with helping those who you can

Yet you are not the Potter, you are only a woman or a man

It's the Lord who gives to those when He feels they need

When you constantly support their habits, you're only supporting their greed

If they stop being a friend because you refuse to help them out

Now you've discovered the real person I've been talking about

Remember the Lord blesses those who are humble and give praise

You will feel a weight lifted, and you can now enjoy your days


Ronnie Fletcher

4/21/13

## No Shame in Shedding Tears

Men are taught that it's a sign of weakness to cry

Yet we all have our sadness that we can't explain why

Men are told "You are weak!", if you show emotions or fears

So we hide our feelings, too embarrassed to show our tears

Yet tears are a sign that our emotions are real

But we all fall victim to hiding how we truly feel

While we may not want to show others our pain

The Lord also cries, but we call His tears our rain

When He is angry, we witness His thunder and lightning

As we tremble at the sound, we can only remember how frightening

While men continue to deny that their sadness is a hidden sorrow

What they don't realize is that sadness brings blessings of tomorrow

So don't ever be ashamed, when you're sad just allow a tear

Those who walk with God, know you have His listening ear

The enemy would love for us to think we're too big to cry

But even Jesus shed a tear on the cross, as He asked why

Nobody was greater; nobody ever made more of a sacrifice

If the Lord can shed a tear, then you shouldn't think twice

So the next time you're ashamed, or saddened by your fear

Remember my message, there's no shame in shedding tears

Fletch

2/26/12

46

## Do You Procrastinate?

You are in your season of harvest right now

When you witness God's hand, your reaction is "wow"

Do you remember years ago when you didn't understand your desires?

Yet when you look back now, you wonder who lit up your fire

When you do God's will, he blesses you with much more

Do you realize it was God's hands which picked you from the floor?

Have you ever met those people who are fighting to do something and never get it done?

Are you one of those procrastinators who only looks out for number one?

Do you know someone who always states they need more time?

Acting like they are God's blessing, yet they never have a dime

Your harvest is now, are you one who procrastinates?

How can you lead by example when you ignore your own fate?

The Lord gives you blessings once we've done our own battles with life

You can't lead by example until you experience life's sacrifice

How can someone tell you how to get somewhere they haven't been?

Ignore their advice, because if you follow them, you can't win

Just follow Jesus and watch your blessings begin to unfold

He is the King who will give your life a story to be told

So if you believe, you should walk by faith and not by sight

Then hear Jesus when He states I'm your lite

Ronnie Fletcher

3/17/13

47

# Selfish Stuff

I want you to sit down and think about stuff

If you tally all you've collected, then you'd say that's enough

Yet we continue to buy and collect what we don't need

Is this due to being selfish, or to our own greed?

If you are selfish, then you cannot serve our Lord

Your selfish ways won't allow you to see you're a fraud

Do you realize your biggest joy will come when you help another?

It can be a stranger, or your sister or brother

Do you realize a selfish person only thinks about me, me, me?

Now, you may not realize how selfish you can be

Do you realize the joy when you help without wanting back?

Now this will bring a blessing that no devil can attack

Do you realize that selfish is the person who sits alone?

You may have riches and stuff, but no satisfaction to atone

So, if selfish is a life you choose to live

How can you change your spirit to learn how to give?

Yet the day that you realize you have enough

That will be your blessing when you get rid of your selfish stuff

Ronnie Fletcher

4/28/13

## Your Harvest is White

### (John 4.35-39)

Do you know what Jesus meant when He said this?

Are you one to listen and realize your bliss?

Your harvest is white means live and enjoy the now

Yet you sit and complain about the here and the how

Why do you complain about the silly things in your life?

And fellas, do you remember the day when you wanted her as your wife

Do you complain about your looks or maybe your weight?

Find some old pictures and now you can appreciate

Your harvest is white means enjoy what is given to you

Yet instead of being thankful, you feel like you're owed your dues

Your harvest is white means if you could go back and change your past

I'm sure you'd change a lot of your bad decisions really fast

Your harvest is white means what seems like hard times ain't

If you turned back the clocks, you'd feel really faint

Your harvest is white means enjoy the wealth given today

I'm sure tomorrow would look better if you changed your yesterday

Your harvest is white means thank God you are able to stand

There might come a day when your way of life might not be so grand

Your harvest is white, I can't stress this to you enough

Thank God for your blessings because without Him life would be tough

Ronnie Fletcher

4/28/13

## I've Got Your Back

I had to think about the word spoken today

It was about what the Pastor had to say

She spoke about a light that shines on your face

It was the Holy Spirit who entered my darkened space

When your enemies confront you with their negative word

It's the Holy Spirit who shows them who's absurd

When your enemies feel they want a fight

It's the Spirit who has your back, to show you it's alright

Have you ever wondered why certain people never bother you?

These people see your spirit, which stands behind you like a crew

You have the light that's there for all to see

It's the Holy Spirit giving strength that you thought couldn't be

When strangers look upon you and see the light

It's the Lord showing His presence that everything will be alright

So, on those days when I feel alone or just losing track

It was my Lord who said "Don't worry, I've got your back."

Ronnie Fletcher

4/28/2013

## It's in Our Spirit

Good morning my friends, have you felt the Lord's Spirit?

It's something you can't explain, there are many who can't hear it

We listen with our ears, we believe with our eyes

As we go through life, realizing all of life's lies

When you are given God's Spirit, it lives within you

What you must believe is that the Holy Spirit is true

We are like a lightning rod, designed to receive

While it may seem impossible, it's God Spirit we must believe

Turn and touch someone, and tell them it's in your spirit

While we haven't seen it, it was spoken for us to hear it

When God wills it in you, He places it in your soul

Many people won't believe your vision when they are told

Because people who don't believe, rely on their natural senses

A natural response that only accepts our human defenses

Yet when you receive it in the spirit, it will be yours to come

A vision has been revealed, you know where it's from

If it is meant for you to have, the Spirit will reveal it to you

While others don't see what you see, God will give you your due

So when you receive the word that touches you in spirit

Those goose bumps will touch your soul, while others don't hear it

So when your eyes begin to tear, with tears rolling down your face

Give thanks to our Lord, because His spirit is our grace


Ronnie Fletcher

4/28/13

# Prepare Yourself

Now I want you to think about the lonely ant

Small by nature, a creature that doesn't know "can't"

You see, this little creature was given a powerful gift

When he finds food to store, that's food he can lift

God didn't give any other creature this special power

You see, the ant doesn't worry, as he works every hour

The message the ant sends, is that we must prepare ourselves

Don't worry about yesterday, but go ahead and stock your shelves

As long as you live in your past, you will live behind

So learn from the ants who prepare what they find

The ants store their food while others laugh at their work

We must prepare like the ant, even when others call you a jerk

The problem with people is that we dwell on the past

Haven't you noticed how life passes by so fast?

Did you ever realize that God's plan has already been decided for you?

So why do you seem so unwilling to prepare for what you must do?

Don't worry how things may look strange to the human eye

Stop concerning yourself with haters who might question why

Because when the world questions why God has given you His wealth

Stand up and tell them how you've prepared yourself

Ronnie Fletcher

5/3/13

52

## Do You Understand Your Gift?

Well, we got a message that made our thoughts shift

It was an education about God's gift

We are all given a talent, and some shine like a light

The question was asked, did you understand the message tonight?

You are the vessel that carries God's talent

Do you use your gift, or have you wasted time spent?

We all feel we have a talent that needs a stage

Yet what do some do other than remain in their own cage?

The Lord gives us our gift to do our special deed

So why do you question the vessel that the Lord's hand feeds?

The talent that is given will be needed one day

Will you be ready when the time comes, for your ultimate display?

The talent given to you is yours alone to shine

When God calls for your moment, you won't be hard to find

So stay connected with the Lord, please don't shift

Just remember my question! Do you understand your gift?

Ronnie Fletcher

2/23/14

# The Locusts are Coming

(Exodus 10)

Now let's think of this small insect which is dark green

Although it may look harmless, it's a sight when it is seen

You see, the locust is an insect that might scare you

Because it's never alone, always traveling with a crew

Even in the bible when they came, it was as a swarm

Never allowing its path to be too big from its harm

Even if some were killed, it just allowed the others to destroy

So when you angered one, you knew his friends weren't a toy

They were never concerned about losing their way

The locusts traveled in packs, ready for any day

We need to learn the way of the locusts, yes indeed

Because if we travel with other Christians, our spirit would feed

In the bible, the locust would come and darken the skies

People were scared, and they didn't know why

More scared of the locust than any army or sword

Because people didn't understand the force of our Lord

When Jesus allowed himself to be killed, so we could live

While He hung on the cross, He asked His Father to forgive

Because while His blood poured, why didn't Christians swarm to His aid?

An unknown answer, as Jesus' life began to fade

If only the Christians could have been the  locust of spring

Then their voices could have yelled "the Christians are coming!"

Ronnie Fletcher

5/5/13

## Alone

Good morning you, I have a question made for you

Did you ever think that this was a path you could do?

Are you someone who is kind hearted and caring to others?

Or are you someone who smothers their sisters and brothers?

Is waking up in the morning, by yourself, something you condone?

Do you feel you're a good person, yet you're alone?

In the bible, Jacob was the son of Abraham, who ended up by himself

Even though he had all the ladies, cattle and great wealth

How can someone as nice as you have no one by your side?

Even when your heart aches, it's your pain you're trying to hide

How can someone be faithful all throughout their life?

Even though you might be loyal, you have a cheating wife

How can someone be so forgiving, and listen to others on the phone?

Even though you desire another's company, you still remain alone

Have you ever realized life is but a moment to enjoy?

Instead of trying to live up to standards, you should learn to have joy

Are you one to always gossip and keep up with others' drama?

If you listen to those so called friends, they call you a nosey mama

So, tonight when you decide to call someone on the phone

Ask yourself why you are without any love, and left all alone

Ronnie Fletcher

5/5/13

# Now I Understand

(1 Corinthians 14:14)


Do you understand that when you are blessed it is through our Lord?

If He allows you to speak to a deaf ear, just stand and applaud

Although you understand His message when He speaks to your spirit

It's for you to translate to those who can't hear it

Now this blessing is a blessing that He reveals to a very few

It can be as a bi-lingual or just a messenger made for you

Have you ever heard that stranger just smile and give you a word?

Wondering who is he to speak, made you think how absurd

Did a stranger ever tell you something that later came true?

In 1 Corinthians 14-21 God clearly says the stranger's word is for you

Some things that happen in life will make no sense

Yet without understanding or being stubborn, it causes us to be on our defense

Allow the spirit to work, the spirit that He placed in you

It's a feeling that very few will understand, as they watch what you do

Tell all who ask, why you smile from ear to ear

Say because the Lord is with me, as you shed a tear

Tell all to give themselves to only Him, as He takes your hand

As the spirit lifts their hearts, hear them confess (now I understand)


Ronnie Fletcher

5/9/13

# A Good Hurt

Now I want you to think about how you felt hurt

Was it from the pain of another or from chasing a skirt?

Now I want you to remember how you felt the pain

Was it from someone being honest when your eyes made it rain?

Now I want you to think of who broke your heart

Was it from losing them or you being afraid of a new start?

The Lord will take you to a place known as hurt

But He won't hurt you as you feel buried in the dirt

The Lord will show you that before you can run you must walk

But He won't hurt you, so don't listen when others talk

The Lord might give you some hurt to awaken your soul

But He won't hurt you; sometimes you need to be reminded of what you've been told

There will be times that you feel He has put you through some drama

This will be the Lord reminding you that you will always need mama

Don't worry about the lover or the friend who left you for another

The Lord said "cling to me my child, and you will need no other"

Did you ever meet that person you felt they are the one?

While you gave your heart, they were just having fun

While you felt devastated, while you felt abandoned in the dirt

It was God who lifted you and to show you it was  a good hurt

Ronnie Fletcher

5/16/13

## Maybe You're the Problem

Good morning, another gift as you awaken today

You've been gifted that your eyes have sight for another day

Are you one who takes for granted all of your gifts?

As you stand to walk, I've allowed your legs the strength to lift

Are you one who takes for granted what you have from me?

As your eyes opened, I've allowed your eyes the ability to see

Are you one who admires what others have been given?

As you neglect what you have, whose fault is it how you are living?

Are you one who spends their time talking about another?

While you continue to look outward, yet it's your blessing that you smother

Instead of admiring what someone else has every day

Try looking inside yourself before your blessings begin to decay

Instead of criticizing what someone else does in their time

Try looking inside yourself; that's where you will find the crime

Instead of being jealous of the blessings of a friend

Try looking at yourself before your blessings come to an end

Instead of whining about what another has done to you

Try looking at yourself; it's there that you'll find your just due

Let's try something new; let's be grateful for our gifts

As you learn to look inside, your outlook on life might shift

Ronnie Fletcher

5/19/13

## Keep Your Vision

We go through life with the hope of change

Now this is a vision we should never exchange

The Lord places His vision of where you will be

Yet it's the Devil who enters to say this can't be

If we go through life always doubting our hope

Then the Devil has won; He's placed your neck in his rope

These dreams that you have are the Lord's promise to you

Yet you find it easier to complain or dismiss what is true

Now what people don't understand is the Lord blesses in His time

It may seem like forever, but losing faith is the real crime

A true believer knows God will deliver on His word

Yet because it doesn't happen as fast, some feel this is absurd

If you allow negative surroundings to change who you are

Then you've allowed the Devil to take the wheel of your car

Take a picture with your mind, of the promise you were given

Believe what God has promised, and change how you're living

The Lord gave you a vision, and it will come to pass

No matter what the problem, you must believe it won't last

That dream that you have; the one that lights up your spirit

Just believe it will happen, it was God's hand that let you live it

Ronnie Fletcher

5/19/13

## The Devil's Waiting On You

You have a purpose, which has been placed by our lord

One you should complete; it's your fulfillment that we applaud

Now the devil has a plan that you might not understand

His purpose is to stop the plan of every woman and man

You see, the mightier the purpose, the stronger he will stand

He understands what your goal is, that's why he has his plan

The devil does not have to kill you; it's his goal to block your purpose

What may seem like confusion might turn into his circus

You may not understand that path that you are on

It's a road that is toward Jesus, whether it is moonlight or the break of dawn

Understand this won't be easy; life never is

When the devil brings his roadblocks, tell him to mind his biz

You will find people or circumstances that might seem too heavy

But as long as you stay connected, it's God's spirit that you levy

Stay focused on your path, some might say that you are driven

Just look to the Lord to direct how you are living

Now don't think that you won't be led off of the beaten track

Just remember God's promise; He said "Son I got your back"

While the devil is strong, he knows he can't win

When he sees the light of Jesus, he'll know where you've been

Ronnie Fletcher

5/27/13

## Who Are You?

Sit down, my friends, because this message is deep

I want to touch your spirit, even when you sleep

This question I have is one that will be told

It's a question about your strength; it's one about your soul

Now the question I ask is are you a fighter?

Or are you one to back down when you feel the opposition is mightier?

You will be tested; you will have others question your brain

Are you a fighter, or are you one who avoids life's pain?

Because a fighter isn't pretty, but he will draw the line

And when you cross their path, they will tell you when things aren't fine

The reason I ask is because the Lord gives us all a role

Whether it's to lead, or it's to fight until the story is told

The Lord knew Moses was a leader, and chose him to lead

He was chosen to make an ark with lots of animals to feed

The Lord knew Joshua was a fighter, with a soul to defend

He had the spirit of a warrior, who would fight to the bitter end

A leader is someone who can take charge without delay

Knowing what is needed on any given day

Now, if you are a leader and a fighter, who takes command

You, my friend, are blessed, and will lead any man

So I ask the question, as your path may soon be revealed to you

Are you ready for your walk; are you ready for what God has planned for you?

Ronnie Fletcher

5/27/13

## Do You Understand the Blood?

Good evening my fellow sinners who deny the love of Christ

Do you realize how much the Lord gave with His only son's sacrifice?

We're talking about a loving God who sent His only son

And when they crucified Jesus, the devil felt he'd won

Yet the devil and those non believers didn't realize on that day

That it was the blood of Jesus that gave the world a new way

Throughout the bible we hear of how there was always a sacrifice

And through the lamb's blood, we all remain protected by Christ

Just like the eve when the Lord told Moses to place lamb's blood at his people's door

So when the angel of death came, he knew death wasn't needed there anymore

The blood of the lamb has always symbolized the blood Jesus shed

Even with His dying breath, His spirit wasn't ever considered dead

On Sundays when you take communion and you take of the bread

Are you a true believer, or are you one who just wants to be fed?

And on Sunday when the pastor offers you to drink of the blood

Are you a true believer, or just someone who should've stuck their head in the mud?

If you read the bible it tells us in 1 Corinthians 11-29

Don't come to God's house acting like everything is really fine

Because if you take part in the communion and you're living a lie

Then you will be the one who suffers until the day you die!

Ronnie Fletcher

6/5/13

# Memory Lane

Now let's go down a darkened street called memory lane

Do you remember your past, do you remember your pain?

Now let's think about your troubled, mixed up past

You didn't understand how you were allowed to last

God stepped in to save you from your bumpy road

Did you think your problems were only yours to unload?

Let's travel down that road with the crooked friends

You know, the people who felt they had to rob to survive, way back when

Let's continue down the road to look for those troubled times

Do you remember how you were when you committed those crimes?

God stepped in to save you from your sorry, misled self

His plan was already in motion to give you His wealth

Let's continue down the road, with the people at your side

You know, the ones who disappear when trouble doesn't let you hide

God stepped in to save you from your path of destruction

To place you under His wing, He placed you under construction

So no matter your problem, no matter your pain

If you lose sight of God, then take a trip down memory lane

Ronnie Fletcher

6/9/13

## Favor Ain't Fair

Hello people, I mean those who have favor

Do you realize that others don't seem to like your flavor?

You've been given God's blessing without doing a thing

Yet it shows in your presence, the smile that you bring

Favor ain't fair, it's not something you've earned

All through your life, you may have felt you were burned

When God gives you favor, He gives you things for His reason

This is a blessing that He gives, no matter the season

Do you wonder why people look at you in disgust?

It's because they see your life and your blessings, without a fuss

Why him Lord? Does he receive your favor every day?

As we wonder why he refuses to even pray

Yet he goes through life acting like he doesn't care

It's when we realized, favor ain't fair

Ronnie Fletcher

6/9/13

64

## You've Got 40 Days

Now people always worry about the unforeseen

When things don't go their way, they cry out, "Why are you so mean?"

Now people always blame God for what they didn't get

Yet do they realize if God changed it, your path would be one of regret?

Instead of blaming someone for what you didn't receive

Change your thinking and realize the Lord doesn't deceive

Now if God came to you and said you have 40 days

Could you change who you are, could you change your ways?

If you were given a timetable to get your life together

Could you fix your path, could you prepare for the weather?

Too many times people have been given a sign or a warning

Only to ignore it, yet they cry when they lose all their belongings

God will use a sinner to warn a sinner of his path

Knowing a sinner can relate to another who does his math

40 was the number used for the people to pay

Because they disobeyed his word, they were led astray

No matter where you've been, just repent your ways

The Lord has a plan, what would you do if He said you've got 40 days?

Ronnie Fletcher

6/9/13

## Women

Good morning ladies, I was touched by our Lord

He revealed His message for all to applaud

Now I want you to understand why you have so many demands

You were given all at birth, you were created through man

God created man; He gave him control from the start

Yet He removed you from the man, so you could do your part

When woman came to life, she was given all she needed

While man was lonely, your presence was greeted

What's sad about a woman is that she's always been supportive

Yet she seems to find a man who doesn't know how to live

What's sad is that a woman is always there to help a man

Yet she seems to find the one who never understands

It could be a husband, a son, or a male friend

Yet it's the same old story to the bitter end

What's even sadder is when you decide to reach out

The one you try to help doesn't know what you are talking about

What's even sadder still, is when you cry out for a helping hand

It's not very often that help comes from a man

Sons and husbands always lean on you for support

Yet do they understand you're a woman, not a fort?

Take care of yourself; treat yourself to a good life

Once you understand who you are, that will end your sacrifice

Ronnie Fletcher

6/13/13

# Thy Will Be Done

Listen everybody, to the message today

It's very powerful, and we must continue to pray

Now, for some people it might not be fun

Yet in the bible, it states "Thy will be done"

Now this phrase is about a connection with the Lord

So bow your heads, because it's a message you should applaud

So many people go to church to speak their pain

Only when in trouble, or when their spirit has been drained

Yet like a phone call, you can't speak and not listen

The Lord knows who is fake, and He knows a true Christian

Once you speak to God, do you also listen for His voice?

Because He is the only one who gives you a real choice

You must learn to pray for everything that you need

Not for what you feel you want, not for your selfish greed

He wants you to live as it is in Heaven

As it states in the bible, the world was finished on day seven

So when you realize it's through His connection you should live

Prayer is the only way Our Father can forgive

He never said life would be easy; never said it would be fun

Yet when you kneel and pray, Thy will be done

Ronnie Fletcher

6/15/13

## There is a King in You

In the bible, there is a man known as Abraham

He was married to Sarah, he seemed humble as a lamb

This man wanted children, but it was his wife who was unable

Now he could have wandered, yet he stayed faithful, in his stable

One day God came to him and revealed He would bless him with a son

He questioned God "how, if my wife is too old to have one?"

There was a rumble from the sky, on this sunny day

Never question my word, just remember what I say

Abraham went to Sarah and told her of God's word

She laughed and said, "my husband, you know I am too old, haven't you heard?

Please, my husband, have this child that He promised with another

I am not the one that God wanted to be a mother"

Years later, although Abraham did give a child to another

God's angels came again and said, "Your wife Sarah will be a mother"

Abraham rejoiced as he cried out to his only wife

"The Lord promised that your body would produce a new life"

What people don't realize, was that Abraham did all God asked him to do

His word was spoken, "My son, there is a King in you

You have lived many years, you've had much frustration

Yet you will be King, and you will be King of all Nations

Ronnie Fletcher

6/15/13

## Love It Or List It

Now this message has so many meanings to me

As we reflect on our lives, we ask "how could this be?"

We seem to love what we have settled for

When God has a bigger picture than we could ever endure

Are you willing to take a chance and change your life?

This might hurt! This might feel like you've taken a knife

Now Jesus said "I am the light; all must pass through Thee"

Are you willing to sacrifice the habit of me, me, me?

Now you've become comfortable in the way that you live

How soon you forget, how you were told how to forgive

Aren't you tired of waiting on that special woman or man?

It's time to list them; it's time to take a stand

Because when you have faith, when you follow the Lord's light

What you believed you could love, now seems out of sight

You've lived with the excuses; you've heard all of the lies

Love it or list it, and give your faith to the skies

Because as long as you live, and you question your fate

It's the faith that you question, in your sorry state

Haven't you wondered why nothing seems to fit?

It's because the Lord awaits, for you to love it or list it


Ronnie Fletcher

7/7/13

## A Game You Don't Want to Lose

Ok people, I want you to think about this

It's like a game of football, are you willing to take the risk?

The devil is watching, he's slowly taking his time

Getting ready to play you, like an old nursery rhyme

Like a coach after a game, he makes the team study the others

The devil plots your moves against your sisters or your brothers

Pay attention to your surroundings, as doors will soon close

While you thought you had it figured out, the devil is under your nose

He will tempt you with the things that he knows get your attention

While you feel his comfort, he's changed your whole direction

He is not going to tempt you with things that just don't matter

Only your weakness in having faith will cause your life to splatter

But if you give your attention and your focus to the Lord

Only then will he deploy his angels to your aid while you applaud

The devil watches from below, waiting for you to give in to sin

Weakness in us all, is a fate that we surely cannot win

But if we ask for mercy and give the Lord our heart

He will raise our spirit to give us a brand new start

So take heed to the game, because the bell is about to ring

Put on your game face, so you can wear your championship ring

Ronnie Fletcher

7/14/13

## Are You Ready for Your Blessed Season?

Well, well, now do you realize what God has given?

Do you take for granted, have you been labeled a heathen?

Who are you to sit and judge for no reason?

I am here to tell you, the Lord will change your season

Now don't look around at how others rant and rave

Just give thanks that you aren't a captured slave

Now don't turn your nose up at how others are living

Just give thanks for what you have been given

We all have desires to one day see better times

So do you save, or do you waste your nickels and dimes?

When your season comes, you won't be able to understand

But I hope you have enough sense to thank God's hand

Too many of us think that we are owed a good life

Without any reason, we blame a husband or a wife

But if you ever sit down and realize what we have been given

It might change your concept and your way of living

Because it's God's hand that allows us to do things without reason

And that's because He is getting you ready for your blessed season

Ronnie Fletcher

7/14/13

## Remember When You Didn't Have a Clue

Alright everyone, it's time you stopped and listened

Are you a true believer; are you a born again Christian?

My question is: Are you grown when you turn twenty one?

Or are we children who feel grown up and ready for fun?

I'm here to tell you that twenty one is only a digit

And you aren't grown until you have the Holy Spirit

When you had a problem that you felt was too big for two

And you found the answer; do you realize **He blessed you**?

Now you might feel like you are old enough to handle yourself

But you haven't grown until the Lord gives you His wealth

You didn't know how you always seemed to find a way out

**He blessed you**, even when you had nothing but doubt

If the Lord gave you things you wanted, at your time

Think back to where you'd be, probably without a dime

He gives you what you want, when He knows that you are ready

Not when you ask, but when He knows your faith is steady

I am here to tell you to believe in the Lord, and you will see

Just look around, I'm here to tell you what He did for me

You don't need anyone to show you how the Lord has helped you

Just think back to the moments you didn't have a clue

Ronnie Fletcher

7/17/13

## My question is: Have You Ever?

Have you ever wondered how you would ever get away?

It was a close call, but God blessed you today

Have you ever wondered why things always happen to you?

It's because your path is chosen, and there is nothing you can do

Have you ever wondered why there is always something going on?

Even when you're weak, the Lord's hand made you strong

Have you ever wondered why you've always felt so out of place?

It's because God has a purpose, to keep you in His space

Have you ever paid attention to the things going on around you?

Yet you still seem puzzled, like you haven't got a clue

Have you ever cried out stating I can't take this pain?

Yet God blessed you with His touch; your eyes felt His rain

Have you ever wondered how you would ever make it through?

Your path has already been chosen, as the Lord walks with you

Yet as you go through life, your attitude is I'd never

As the Lord continues to bless you, my question is: Have you ever?


Ronnie Fletcher

7/22/13

# Heather

Attention everybody! Now people please pull up your chair

Sadness isn't permitted, so please don't you dare

If you never knew perfect, then you didn't know Heather

She had a peaceful disposition, no matter what the weather

I never met anyone who seemed so at peace with a smile

She was always so kind, whether you were an adult or a child

While we all never want to leave this place called Earth

Heather was so precious, she never realized her worth

So I want everyone to hold back the sadness today

Heather had a meeting with the other angels on Sunday

She realized the Lord had called this meeting to order

Sad about her departure are not only her friends, but her daughters

But we must realize that she hasn't left us at all

When the Lord calls out, we must answer that call

He has a new life for Heather up in heaven

So He made himself clear, report here on day seven

She always remained with a smile on her face

Never showing her pain or sadness of this place

So people dry your eyes, please wipe your tears

I give thanks for being part of her life for many years


Ronnie Fletcher

7/17/13

## God Approved You

Today I have to ask you: How you feel?

Are you a person of wisdom, or just a person of sex appeal?

Now before you answer, I want you to realize

You were created in God's image, which means any size

When will you stop trying to be someone you're not?

God created us all for His purpose, or have you forgot?

The things that you wish for may not be meant for you

So why, I ask you, do you try to do something that you can't do?

What God has for you will be given to you in His way

Yet you struggle to achieve what isn't meant for you today

The road to His glory is already set in His stone

So why do you question the fact that He has you alone?

When God is ready, you will find your own path

How long before you realize how to do the simple math?

Stop trying to reach for the things you can't possibly do

And remember it's your time, God has already approved you!

Ronnie Fletcher

8/4/13

# I Wonder How Long?

How long are you going to walk in the dark?

Are you a person who remains a dog without a bark?

How long are you going to put the blame on another?

Are you a person who is jealous of your own sister or your brother?

How long are you going to simply live to just get by?

Are you one without a cause; are you one who just wants to cry?

How long will you allow others to steal your thunder?

Are you one who just complains, or are you one who often wonders?

How long will you be neglectful of what's given to you?

Are you one who squanders blessings, then wonders what to do?

How long before your loved ones get tired of your actions?

Are you one to blame all others; are you the big distraction?

How long do you think your family and friends will stand by you?

While you cause them pain with the hurtful things you do?

How long will you be a burden on someone else's life?

The pain you cause to others goes deeper than any knife

I am here to tell you that your loved ones' patience is running out

Soon the day will come when others won't hear your shout

Get yourself together, it is time to stand up strong

Before you lose those people who put up with you for so long!

Ronnie Fletcher

8/15/13

## It's God's Hand That Determines Our Fate

Good morning everyone, as the sun rises into the skies

As you rise from bed, as you open up your eyes

It's a new day for all whom the Lord has blessed today

Yet you still dwell on problems that happened yesterday

Many people cry inside about something in their past

Some things might seem minor; a pain you thought wouldn't last

Not everyone can recover from some things that happened before

Yet they carry this burden instead of closing that painful door

But if you would put behind you this trauma of your past

You could move on with a better life that could change so fast

The Lord never promised anyone that life would be easy from the start

Now, if you hope to achieve God's plan, then you must do your part

Life is like playing cards; you can only play with what you are dealt

When you allow the Lord to work, it's His blessings that are felt

Whether you are from a broken home, or you are an abused child

Whether you are misunderstood, or maybe someone took away your smile

We all go through things before we can get where we need to be

And I know I am not the only one who has asked the Lord "Why me?"

Yet when He answers, and for some it may feel too late

Remember it's Gods hand that determines our true fate

Ronnie Fletcher

8/15/13

# The House

The message today is for all to stay in

No matter how sunny, outside is where troubles begin

When you were a child and you wanted to go outside

It was the devil's voice that knew how to hide

For all whom are blessed, it's the house that protects

The devil is a liar, as his power is neglect

He can't get to you, while you're in God's house

So he will try to get close like a women's blouse

He will tempt you; he will offer you your desires

As he reaches for your spirit, beware of his fire

The Lord built His house to give His children a shelter

Yet there are those who do not know what God's house is for

The Lord blessed you, yet you allow the devil in

Only because you went outside, a place you shouldn't have been

Now you're outside and trying to get back in the house

Whining about your problems, squeaking like a mouse

Beware of temptation, for there is a price you will pay

Remember my warning, and stay in the house today

Ronnie Fletcher

8/28/13

# Temptation

Now people, this is a word that may lead you astray

While some may fall victim, others give Satan his way

So many of us have our moments when the flesh is weak

As we fall to temptation, allowing the devil to speak

While many have asked the Lord to deliver them from temptation

Do we really want to feel the emptiness or isolation?

As we resist temptation, we might find ourselves alone

Are you ready to be strong? An action the devil won't condone

Temptation is what the devil uses on our body and souls

Yet we fall victim to what's offered while our weakness unfolds

We may try to fight off temptation, which means saying NO

Can you handle rejection; are you ready for this new show?

The devil brings temptation because he knows your song

Is it your soul that's in denial? Have you made Satan that strong?

Do you remember when you tried to fast for 40 days?

Were you able to last, or were you tempted in so many ways?

Did the devil come to you with his own flirtation?

Offering what he could; do you remember his temptation?

He knows the flesh is weak; he knew you wouldn't last

Sad that he was right, because you failed at your task

But if you just stand up, try to deny his flirtation

Then that would be the day you denied his temptation

Ronnie Fletcher

9/2/13

## Who Are You Listening To?

Now I want you to think about this question at hand

Do you listen to the spirit, or listen to a man?

You are judged by others, based on your word

Are you careful about your actions, or does this seem absurd?

Now you have moments when you must make a choice

Do you seek a person's word, or do you seek the Lord's voice?

Have you given yourself to our Lord and savior?

Or are you a victim of the devil who offers any flavor?

How can you hear the Lord if you don't know Him?

Yet you trust your friends whether it's Bill, Bob, or Jim

Take time out of your day to surrender yourself to our Lord

This will change your life, a move your soul will applaud

Why do you follow the devil's voice? He always steers you wrong.

Yet you follow his voice because you thought you were so strong

What about the little voice that warned you not to stray?

You remember, as you refused to follow him today

How long will you make excuses about your sorry life?

Since you chose to cut your chances with the devil's knife

Think about your next decision, when you don't have a clue

Before you make a move, ask who are you listening to?

Ronnie Fletcher

9/10/13

## Are You a Runaway?

Do you realize the things that happen every day?

Are you paying attention, or do you run away?

When things go wrong and you seem to blame another

Are you a runaway? Who always seeks their mother?

We all have problems; this is something we must learn

Yet when God gives us the answer, the devil wants his turn

Are you a prisoner, one who is locked up inside of you?

Always complaining about another, never knowing what to do

The devil wants you; he's very patient for your soul

While you run away from God, it's Satan's plan you unfold

Are you a runaway, always seeking more but giving less?

God is the only answer, so why do you run away, rather than be blessed?

Now you can run, but when will you realize you cannot hide?

Are you a runaway who only lives with foolish pride?

Well, I am here to tell you, it is Jesus waiting for you, with open arms

So, will you run away? Will you set off troubled alarms?

Every day you refuse to give yourself to Christ

Is a day that Satan rejoices about your foolish sacrifice!

Ronnie Fletcher

9/8/13

## How Can You Feel God's Glory?

Hello everyone, I'm sure you have a story

Can you be honest? Can you feel God's glory?

Let's take a moment to see where you've been

Have you lived a loving life, or lived a life of sin?

Now don't be ashamed, we have all made our mistakes

So, what have we done to change? Do you know what's at stake?

We find it easy to talk about other's flaws

Yet when we look in a mirror, do we put our mistakes on pause?

Do we only seek God when we have a problem or mistake?

How many times did you ask for forgiveness? How much can God take?

It's easy to pass judgment on how others try to live

So, tell me, are you a phony Christian who can't seem to forgive?

Because until you find a mirror, until you change your story

How can you be a leader? How can you feel God's glory?

Ronnie Fletcher

9/15/13

## Just Pray

The sermon today had a strong message indeed

It was one of wisdom; it was of the devil's greed

The message today informed us that the Lord wants us to pray

While a powerful word was delivered, we just listened in church today

We were told of how we are tested on our faith throughout life

Never too old to be tested, never too young for Satan's knife

While the Lord seeks our prayers, Satan wants your soul

When your faith is weakened, Satan tries to grab his hold

If God allows you to fail, it's only because He wants you to pray

Just when you thought all was lost, the Lord saves the day

Take Jonah, who jumped into the sea, rather than face his fear

Yet the Lord sent him a whale to protect him as he prayed thru his tears

Oh, and let's not forget the three young men who disputed praying to a statue

When the king sentenced them to burn, it was God who said "I got you"

We all have our moments when we lose our faith and hope

Those are the times you need to pray and learn how to cope

If we would just stop worrying about our problems and pray

We would then understand the powerful message of today

The Lord only asks that we live by faith and not by sight

How long will it take you to learn how to pray tonight?

Ronnie Fletcher

9/15/13

# A Real Man

Good morning fellas, I have a message for you

It may seem hard, but it's an understanding for two

The message that I have is one you might not like

It's one about being responsible, not taking a hike

Do you remember when you met the lady of your heart?

Did you promise her the world; did you promise her a fresh start?

Do you remember the way you felt about her smile?

Did you promise to be faithful, did you father a child?

Well, she believed the lines that came from your voice

Little did she know, she'd become your victim with no choice

Many men become fathers, yet they also became liars

While the woman gave birth, their dreams were set on fire

Now today a lot of mothers have children whose fathers are a wreck

Instead of being a real man, he's become a pain in the neck

Now today a lot of women have to beg for child support

From the one who once loved her, she's forced to take him to court

So fellas, if you're not ready to stand up to give from the heart

Be careful what you ask of her, from the start

Most women want a relationship with a person in command

The spirit of a lion, are you a real man!

Ronnie Fletcher

9/26/13

## Can You Afford Not To Pray?

Last night I said a prayer to my Father above

It was a prayer of forgiveness, a prayer of love

I wanted to acknowledge the blessings given to me

As I knelt down to pray, my soul felt so free

I closed my eyes after my prayer to the Lord

Not forgetting His touch, a move no one could afford

Yet I woke up this morning with tears on my face

Not understanding what took place in my lonely space

I wiped my face, yet the tears continued to fall

So I only could pray, without any understanding at all

We often live without ever giving thanks to Thee

How long before you realize, nothing in life comes for free

So I decided to reach out to a stranger today

Without knowing his name, I asked "did you pray?"

I continued my walk seeking another stranger, by chance

Not knowing my steps, yet the Lord knew in advance

Yet you believe you know it all, you think you have life figured out

Think about my question! Or do you even know what I am talking about?

We may all have dreams, we make plans where we will be

As I Look to the skies and ask the Lord to forgive a sinner like me

Because until you surrender yourself to our Lord

You will continue your walk blindly,on a path you can't afford


Ronnie Fletcher

10/7/13

# The Fisher of Men

There was a story in the bible about Galilee

It was about a stranger that many couldn't see

As he stood by and watched several men try to fish

He watched them struggle with their empty nets and a wish

Now these men were fishermen, yet they couldn't catch a thing

Yet this stranger continued to watch to see what their struggles would bring

Each time they cast their nets, the results remained the same

Frustrated and angry, but they didn't know who to blame

The stranger yelled out "place your nets on the other side"

With nothing left to lose, except for foolish pride

They did as Jesus told them, and to their surprise

Their nets came back filled with fish of every size

Jesus also used His fishermen to spread His word

Tell all who will listen, even those who call you absurd

Now, this story still holds true to this very day

It's not enough to just believe, we must ALL learn Jesus's way

To be a fisher of men is to be one who truly believes

Spread the word of Jesus Christ, with nothing up your sleeves

We must learn the word, read a scripture every day

This all starts with faith, and the ability to pray

Ronnie Fletcher

10/9/13

## God So Loved the World

### John 3:16

We go through life telling others of our love

Do you know the power of the word "love" from above?

When you look at your loved one and express how you feel

Does the emotion of your heart spin your head like a wheel?

So why I ask, is this the only feeling that causes you to react?

Just because you're in love, doesn't mean they should have your heart attack

Do you really know the power of love is more than we know?

Are you willing to surrender; How far would you go?

Now, the love that God speaks of, it's one of sacrifice

So I must ask the question, would you roll the dice?

Many of us want the love we give, and hope it's received

Yet, when we get hurt, our emotions feel deceived

God's meaning of love has no boundaries; No need to think twice

When we think of God's love, we should think of a great sacrifice

So, if you love someone, it should be no question from the start

Love without expectations, only love with a pure heart

When you love something or when you have love for someone

This may cause your mind to lose focus; it may cause your heart to run

But God's love is one that's so powerful, He's made himself clear

When others questioned His love, he responded "don't you dare"

He created all; He created everything from rocks to a pearl

Yet God gave His only son, because God so loved the world

So today, when you say I love you, know what you're saying

Our God gave His only son; you should be on your knees praying

Ronnie Fletcher

10/10/13

## Trust

Today's message was about the spirit of fear

For those who are Christians, you claim you can hear

Today we learned that we need to confess

While we live for the moment, we live in the wilderness

Now pull up a chair, I think you need to sit down

This message is clear, the bishop wasn't fooling around

The bible tells us that we shouldn't have fear

Yet when this message was delivered, our concerns became clear

You should fear your future will become impacted from your past

Learn from your mistakes, thank God if you last

Your fear should be that you don't accomplish God's goals

How long will you refuse to do as you are told?

Fear will always be around waiting for you to let him in

In case you didn't know, Satan is fear with a grin

If you ever decide to have any fear at all

It should be the fear of not allowing the Lord's blessing to call

Because, if you leave this Earth without trusting in Thee

Then you have allowed fear to rob you of your destiny

We all have a plan, yet we allow fear to get to us

The message is simple, just have faith and trust

Ronnie Fletcher

10/14/13

## Treat a Stranger Like Your Brother

Good morning my Lord, as I have been awakened by Thee

Not knowing my future, I am grateful you've blessed me

Today I was awakened by your spiritual word

It was an education for many, yet your message wasn't heard

You see, we all have our problems, our own cross to bear

How often  we struggle, yet we refuse to hear?

We've all heard the story of how the Son of God carried the cross

Yet when we have a problem, we seem to be at a loss

Throughout the bible, the Lord instructed us to come to Thee

Yet we'd rather blame and complain, and ask "how could this be?"

When we encounter a problem, it's so we can come before our Lord

While many have foolish pride, they cannot even afford

So you go to church, and you've read the good book

Have you tried to be humbled? Do you know how you look?

Yet you still want God's blessing, while you wear guilt on our face

God gave His only son, what have you done to earn the Lord's Grace?

Why don't you try something new? Try to help another

If Jesus can reach out, then why can't you treat a stranger like your brother?

Ronnie Fletcher

10/27/13

## The Ultimate Relationship

Now I want you to think about this message today

It's very important that we learn how we should pray

The message today is about your relationship with our Lord

We need to give thanks, we need to stand and applaud

You must have a relationship, we must acknowledge His hand

Not only when we have a problem, that's not God's plan

Why do we only call on GOD when we have a need?

Whether we have a desire, or a moment of greed

Could this be the reason the Lord lends a deaf ear?

We feel He doesn't answer, we feel He doesn't care

IS your relationship with God  one of compromise

How can you expect a miracle of faith, when you live a life of lies?

Many people live their lives as if it's a game show

Hoping for a prize from a God they don't know

How long will you hope for the blessings of Thee?

Without having a real relationship with God Almighty

This might scare you because this will sting like a whip

Take time out of your busy life to form the ultimate relationship

Ronnie Fletcher

10/27/13

## Mix it Up

Wake up everyone, because there is a message for today

Don't lie around, just drop to your knees and pray

The word today is that all of us need to mix it up

Now this message might cause your spirit to erupt

My Lord spoke to me about a simple milkshake

This might seem weird, but wait until you hear what's at stake

Now I want you to think about when you hear the word

Are there times when you feel the message wasn't truly heard?

I want you to think about when a farmer plants his seeds

Some locations will grow plants, other locations will grow weeds

I want you to think about when you buy an energy drink

All the ingredients are there, but did you mix it up, or just drink?

You must learn to mix faith with the word you receive

Without mixing faith with the message, it becomes hard to believe

It's not enough to believe, we must have faith in the word

Ask questions, if you don't understand, but be clear on what you've heard

We must learn to allow faith to guide our sight

When you truly believe, everything else will be alright

Ronnie Fletcher

10/29/13

## Reach Out

Mark 3:5

Good morning everyone who lives a life of fear

I want you to pay attention; it's time for you to hear

Today I was given a special message for those who have doubt

The Lord spoke through the Bishop; His message stated "reach out"

How long will you live within the circle you call "safe"?

The Bishop yelled "reach out, if you truly have faith"

It's easy for people to say I can't do something I am not used to

The Bishop yelled "reach out! if you want to reach the blessings for you

The Lord said "it won't be easy!" yet the challenge is set

Are you willing to reach out, or will you live a life of regret?

The blessings for you may not come in your time of need

But God does things in His way and throughout time; He has His own speed

It may take more time for your blessings to be realized, in your life

Reach out for what you want; are you willing to make a sacrifice?

You've lived your life to this point complaining or always expecting more

Reach out for what you want, don't allow your blessing to walk out the door

When you reach out, you might stretch your arms until it hurts

These are the challenges in life, as your body sends out your alerts

Reach out of your norm; this will truly hurt for a while

When will you realize some pain will be worth a golden smile?

What might seem hard at first, might surprise you in the end

Reach out from what you're used to, you might touch a golden friend

But if you trust in Thee, and have faith without any doubt

Then you will see the blessings that come from reaching out

Ronnie Fletcher

11/6/13

## Do You Realize What's at Stake?

Our message today was very powerful indeed

While we came for the spirit, it's our minds the Lord feeds

I want you to think about life through all of its temptations

Do you realize nothing comes without you building a foundation?

For example, ladies tonight you look great because you took time

Without you putting in the work, your appearance might be a crime

Just think of a house that is built on the sand

Without the proper foundation, that beautiful house couldn't stand

Now I know we all want the world to give us our way

Anything worth having will require more than one day

Patience is a required skill you learn over the years

There will be many nights and many moments of tears

So dry your eyes, my friends, because the sun will rise

As the Lord blesses you, this should come as no surprise

The sadness you have is because you want more than you give

Just enjoy the moment the Lord has allowed you to live

Any relationship that's worth having will require sweat and tears

Don't run from a misunderstanding; don't run from your fears

What makes you happy may come down a long road you cannot see

Do you really have faith? Do you trust in Thee?

How long have you struggled with situations you didn't understand?

Trust in the Lord as He offers you His extended hand

Reach out to Him; it's a chance you should take

Can you afford not to? Do you realize what's at stake?

Ronnie Fletcher

11/11/13

## I Am With You

As I sat in church today, I listened in amazement

There was a guest pastor who was heaven sent

She spoke about the Lord with such power and grace

While she had our attention, I felt tears roll down my face

She spoke about the members who constantly live a lie

Coming to sing in church, while the word is what they deny

She spoke of the Lord, to all who listen without a clue

While the Lord said "trust in me, as I am with you"

The bible read that we should not live in fear

While many believers come to church, many still cannot hear

She shouted "you had a problem that scared you yesterday"

Pay attention to the word, learn what God has to say

When Satan comes knocking, acting like he is so clever

That's when you turn to Satan with one hand held high and say "whatever"

She shouted "your problems are only bumps in your walk"

Just turn your focus to God, because He hears when you talk

When Satan asks who are you to state "whatever"

You answer, "I am a child of God, now don't you find me clever?"

She spoke of my Lord while quoting what to do

While we listened to her message quoting the bible, stating "I'm with you"

Ronnie Fletcher

11/11/13

## Oh What a Mess

Good evening my friends, oh what a mess

Are you too tired to pray? Are you too guilty to confess?

So, you had a busy day, dealing with some stress

Yet, you can't seem to remember the Lord gave you happiness

Let's go down memory lane, let's visit how the Lord sees your day

He woke you up this morning; did you take time to pray?

You found some clothes in your house to wear

Yet did the Lord get any thanks, that would express you cared?

Now, weren't you able to stand this morning, on your own two feet?

Did you say "thank you Lord" as you found food to eat?

Now all this happened, and that was just the beginning of your day

But you couldn't find a moment to give thanks to the Lord with prayer

So you went on outside to face a brand new day

Yet you find plenty of time to complain, if you don't get your way

So I ask you, my friend, why do you ask for the Lord's blessings?

When you don't give thanks, and you don't have time for confessing?

Why do you feel life owes you anything at all?

When you never say thank you, unless you feel the Lord answers your call

The most important things take very little effort, yet you won't confess

Take a moment to see how you are living! Wouldn't you say "oh what a mess!"

Ronnie Fletcher

11/15/13

# Leave It Alone

Good morning everyone, we heard a strong message today

It was one of wisdom, as we all began to pray

This message was about our faith that God is in control

While some people cried, the message began to unfold

The bishop yelled out! "We all have problems, that's a part of life"

While we scramble to find a solution, some seek a husband or wife

While some decide to reach out through a text or telephone

The bishop yelled "have faith, and leave it alone"

God gives us problems to test our faith in Thee

While you sit and worry, the Lord hears you cry out "how could this be?"

God gives you moments when your eyes shed a tear

While you are worried, the Lord reminds you, I didn't teach you to fear

God gives you rough times to make you reach out to Him

While you hit the panic button, reaching out to Joe or Kim

God watches you blame everyone else, instead of yourself

While you had the solution, you doubted your own wealth

Yet if you truly have faith in our Lord, and stop thinking you're grown

Believe in me, as your God, and as for fear, leave it alone

Ronnie Fletcher

12/8/13

## Do You Understand?

Now pull up a chair and please sit down

I have a message that might knock you to the ground

This message I have is not about a woman or man

It's about life. I hope you understand

We all have a story, we all have expectations

Yet, do you plan for disappointments, do you plan for frustrations?

God gives us problems, God gives us grief

While you label Him our savior, while you label the devil a thief

You must keep it real, because the devil has a story

He waits for your weakness, while God plans for your glory

A woman seeks a man who can lift her if she falls

Whether he has what it takes, Or he has nothing at all

What she sees in him is a spirit she desires

Some men are weak; they don't know their own fire

This is why God gives us all a bumpy road to travel

It's for us to stumble; it's for our problems to unravel

The Lord will test your faith, with frustration in your face

Stand strong and believe, God gave you His grace

So tonight if you meet with a special woman or man

Smile with hope, as God asks "Do you understand?"

Ronnie Fletcher

12/10/13

## He is With Me

Good morning was the introduction to us today

Knowing God's presence gave us the path to God's way

He is with me in the middle of the storm

We seem to be afraid of things out of the norm

He promised that he would be by my side

His presence gives me strength, I choose not to hide

When we find ourselves in the middle of a storm

Afraid we are alone, we become afraid and question norm

Yet God's promise was that He would always be there

Even though I don't see Him, He said have no fear

The Lord's promise wasn't made about you having a house or a car

Material things are only temporary, not going very far

I know He is with me, no matter how difficult the season

Even when I have doubt, even when I don't understand His reason

Yet I have faith, even when I act like I'm grown

While I deal with the storm, I know I am not alone

There will be times that I question how could this be

That's when faith answers, He is with me

The Lord comes through, He lives in trouble and pain

Just when you have doubts, He comes like the rain

So remember, my friends, when you question how could this be

Just raise your head and say "He is with me"

Ronnie Fletcher

12/18/13

## The Best Deal of All

Wake up everyone, no matter how big or how small

The message was clear as we heard the best deal of all

We hear it every day, yet we all seem to forget

Now the message was delivered without any hard feelings or regrets

Do you remember as a child, your desire for a special toy?

Your thrill for Santa, wishes from every girl or boy

Today's celebration of Christmas seems only for presents and gifts

Have you taken a moment to think of whose spirit you could lift?

This time of year has been labeled for heartfelt giving

Most forgetting our savior, most forgetting how they're living

The Lord wants your attention, and for some a change of life

Some will feel His pain, it might feel like you were stabbed by a knife

We always seek forgiveness once we realize we were wrong

If you trust in Jesus, only He can make your spirit strong

So the next time you hear an offer which might make your heart fall

Just trust in Jesus, because that is the best deal of all

Ronnie Fletcher

12/21/13

## My Grace is Enough

Hello everyone, I want you to think about this

His blessings come daily, without you asking or any risks

Yet we all seem to complain. We always seem to want more

Frustrated like children, we seem ready to yell or pound the floor

When we don't get our way, or while we complain about stuff

The Lord responds by saying "my grace is enough"

Now, you may go to church, or you may be one who feels they live right

So how can God say no, when you feel you need His help tonight?

There are times when you feel you have to help others by going out of your way

Doing what you feel is needed, on every God given day

There are other times when you feel you can't take life anymore

Praying for a solution, or asking the Lord to close that hectic door

There may be times when other people's actions have taken you to your end

With nowhere to turn, you thought that person was your true friend

Look around you and pay attention, because you are not alone

Problems and misery will arrive and you won't need to use a phone

There are many roads that you will travel, and be made a fool

Instead of finding the answer, the Lord's answer, you've been overruled

Why is your question "Will the Lord not grant me what I ask"?

Because He knows the outcome, and you can handle this simple task

All through your life, you have complained about simple stuff

When you asked why, the Lord answered "My Grace is enough"

Ronnie Fletcher

12/26/13

100

# Healing

Now I want you to think about this

A time of remorse, a moment to reminisce

Do you only know our Lord when you have an ill feeling?

Or are you one to seek our Lord when you need some healing?

When you need His hand, you feel you need it now

Take a close look in a mirror; your response might be "wow"

When you come to know Jesus, your walk won't be in vain

As people take notice, it will be your smile they'll ask you to explain

Whether you've lost your husband, or the man of your choice

Heart broken and depressed, because you didn't listen to God's voice

What about the person who complains about not having some new shoes?

Ever think about the one who doesn't have a foot? Now do you get the clues?

Do you live on the edge? Do you react without any feelings?

Those are the moments that your spirit needs God's healings

Only the Lord knows the answer as we kneel to the ground

As we seek the Lord's trust, it's our feelings that are spiritually found

Only our actions will show the Lord as we begin to pray

While God seeks obedience, it's our actions of today

So when you feel the spirit, remember that wonderful feeling

As God blesses your walk, your spirit will feel the healing

Ronnie Fletcher

12/29/13

## All Tied Up

A new year has arrived as 2014

Many have made promises to become fit and lean

Yet many have come into this year with their same fears

While they sing and dance, yelling "happy new year"

How many took the time to give thanks for another day?

While the Lord handles their problems, they still refuse to pray

When life reveals its problems, when things seem to erupt

Do you realize it's because our Lord has you all tied up?

I want you to think about how He took away those friends

You know, the ones who lived a troubled life to their very end

I want you to think about that sexy woman or handsome man

The one who didn't care, the one who could never understand

I want you to think about how you lost that job or promotion

It was God who changed your path by causing such a commotion

Look back at while you were tied up and God changed your path

Did you ever give thanks? Have you finally done the math?

The Lord is in control, so thank Him while you sing

Please learn to pay attention, learn to be grateful for the little things

So, I want you to sit down tonight and review your past

Because without the Lord's hand, how long would you last?

Thank Him for His hand as He shows the world your glow

While God shows you favor, it's your spirit that will show

Ronnie Fletcher

1/1/14

## Follow Me

With the message of today we asked "How could this be?"

That's when we heard the Lord's voice say "Just follow me"

While we all go through life chasing hopes and dreams

Facing troubled times, dealing with disappointment, going to the extreme

While we seem willing to climb any mountain to get the gold

Yet, are we willing to know Jesus? Are we willing to do as we are told?

While we are told give the Lord our troubles, because you are not alone

He is there when you call, and you don't even need a cell phone

How many times have you asked the Lord for one more chance?

Yet after He gave your request, you still returned to your same old dance

Instead of seeking material things, instead of blaming Thee

Why don't you try something new? Remember His words "Follow Me"

Jesus said only through Me will you see my father and succeed

Are you one who seeks the Lord only when you have a need?

Since you barley survived your ways and still ask how could this be

Maybe it's time for a change; remember His words "Just Follow Me"

Look at history; look at the world of today

Can't you see God's message? Can't you see the sadness every day?

Why, you ask, does our Lord allow so many to suffer and die?

Maybe we need to just follow Jesus, instead of asking why

Because today we have a chance to change our tomorrow

Or do we stand by and continue to witness endless sorrow?

Ronnie Fletcher

1/9/14

## Be Happy For Me

Hello everyone who have tears in their eyes

I am here with our Father, just look to the skies

While you seem at a loss on this happy day

Listen to my voice because I have something to say

Today is a day that you should all reminisce

Think of our good times, think of the times we will miss

Instead of the phrase "Lord how could this be?"

Keep up my memory, and be happy for me

Now I've left your side, I've left your close space

I've left your world with tears on my face

Our Father has welcomed me home in His arms

Calling His angels, setting off all kinds of alarms

The gates have opened to welcome me here today

My spirit is alive and I've found comfort in a heavenly way

So for all of my family and for all of my friends

There is a heavenly gate where I thought was the end

I thank all of you, but please understand I am free

Don't cry, don't be sad, just be happy for me!

Ronnie Fletcher

1/20/14

## Welcome to Hell

Today's message was a powerful one indeed

It was a word of power, it was something we would need

Today's message gave us a vision into the night

When it was delivered, it gave a blind man his sight

The question was asked, "Do you have a story to tell?"

Are you one who has problems? Have you been living in Hell?

Everyone feels they have a situation that they can't control

Look back at your choices, were you warned how things could unfold?

Don't look to blame someone else for the choices that you've made

Hoping for forgiveness, as your chances began to fade

Look back to what got you to where you are today

Now you're hoping that God will change your unforgiving way

It was you who made the choice, the decision you couldn't tell

That's when you found the sign, that read "Welcome to Hell"

Many go through life feeling they are cursed

Yet do they realize things could always be worse?

So, until you surrender and give God your glory

You will keep repeating the same old sad story

Until you understand and decide on a life that suits Him well

There is a sign outside that states "Welcome to Hell"

Ronnie Fletcher

1/20/2014

## Steps

Good morning everyone who feels they know everything

Some feel they are blessed, while others feel they have nothing to bring

Good morning everyone who feels the world revolves around you

Some feel they are the answer, while others feel they don't have a clue

Good morning everyone who feels they are bigger than life

Those ignoring all the rules, not willing to make that sacrifice

I am here to tell you that taking steps means to follow a process

You can't climb steps until you are willing to confess

Do you remember when you were young and tried to climb the steps too fast?

Remember when you stumbled or tripped but you thought it was a blast?

Do you realize that your path has already been set by our Lord?

So stop trying your way, because this is a move you can't afford

Everything in life requires that we follow a process to achieve

Our steps have already been ordered, when will you believe?

Take those steps before you, because they are part of the process

One step at a time, while you are taught how to confess

So pay attention to those steps, while you begin your climb

Be careful as you go, pay attention to father time

With age comes wisdom, so be careful with each step

Once you learn the process, you will appreciate what you get

Ronnie Fletcher

1/19/14

# The Cross

Good afternoon everyone who doesn't feel like they carry a cross

This is a symbol, it's the sign of a burden or a loss

While you live your life, while you go through everyday pain

Our savior was taken to Calvary, to a place where he was slain

When you think back to how Christ was punished, made to carry that cross

It should make you sad; it should leave you at a loss

Yet He was made to suffer, He carried it as He was ordered

While beaten and punished for unknown crimes, He was beaten to be slaughtered

Now, to this day, we walk around with our cross to wear

Yet are you strong enough to face your burdens without any fear

Could you bear the punishment, would you face what Christ took on?

Punished not for what He did, but because some felt He didn't belong

Yet Christ took on the burden of every boy and girl

While He hung from the cross, for the sins of our world

As Jesus loved us unconditionally and without any fear

He asked his father for our forgiveness, while His body simply hung there

So, I ask you, do you know the meaning of God's grace?

It's the day He gave His only son, while blood ran down His face

While Jesus was crucified in Calvary, Good Friday marks our loss

So remember the true meaning of that symbol called the cross

Ronnie Fletcher

1/27/14

## A Stranger At My Door

Today we heard a story that touched all who heard

We came to hear the sermon, others call it the word

As we listened to the story about clear and unknown danger

This wasn't a normal message; this was about a total stranger

Jesus talked about how we must all learn how to love

How the gates of heaven are open to His Father from above

In the book of Matthew it speaks about caring for those in need

Learn to love and honor, not submit to someone else's greed

Give help to those in need, become the stranger with a smile

Offer your hand as if it was food for a child

The story was about people who opened their house one night

Not concerned what could happen, just doing what was right

This story was about people who came into a dangerous situation

On a highway to hell, only having a life of frustration

Their car started to lose control, almost crashing off to the side

Help came in the form of a stranger, with his arms open wide

This family was welcomed to a house they didn't even know

A house of great warmth welcomed strangers out of the snow

One by one, families were offered help throughout this night

Not understanding their kindness, not understanding what was right

All found help in this house that could only welcome more

They all found out about the stranger at my door!

Ronnie Fletcher

2/2/14

## Change your I to We

The message today was short but direct

It made some feel powerful, while others felt like a wreck

The question was asked to all that would listen

Have you given yourself to Christ, have you become a true Christian?

The reason for this question was clear to those who paid attention

While some people just hang around, there are others we won't mention

The bishop yelled out "people you must change the people in your space"

Those who can't help you, those good for nothing folks in your face

People, you will find people who bring nothing to your table

Those folks just exist, only taking whatever they are able

You'll find those people who always talk about all others

Yet if you really take a look, they're not close to their own sisters and brothers

You'll find those who only hang around to take from you

It's because they are users who have nothing else to do

The Lord wants you to connect with those who can lift you up

Change your life circle and watch how your spirit will erupt

The Lord won't bless you if you never learn how to reach out

Change your environment; come to learn what Christians sing about

How can you stand tall if you're always lying down?

Change your position; it's time to move to a blessed town

Come to a place where your spirit shouts "look at me"

When you meet the spirit of Jesus, He will change your I to We

Ronnie Fletcher

2/5/14

## Reel it In

*Matthew 17-27*

Good morning to those who feel they cannot win

Today's sermon was so powerful, it's hard to begin

The bishop spoke about how we are coming to a new season

While you seem troubled throughout life, do you understand the reason?

I advise you to pay attention, because this is going to get deep

While the bishop spoke, nobody in the house dared to sleep

As his voice rose, he said you must change your dimension

The Lord already has blessed you, yet there's something he failed to mention

You may struggle, at times, always feeling that you came close

Yet things always get away, just when you need them the most

The bishop explained it's because what God has for you

Is so close, yet He wants to make you fight for your just due

The Lord puts your needs into another dimension

So that you can try harder, He makes sure He has your attention

There are times when you feel you must fight for your desires

The Lord never said life was easy, as He increases those fires

So begin your journey; He will give you everything, once you begin

The Lord told Peter I put your needs in one fish, now go reel it in

Ronnie Fletcher

2/10/14

## Your Days

I woke up this morning with emotions all out of place

Trying to understand the tears on my face

As I wiped my eyes, I looked to the sky

Asking my savior the question of why

Before He could answer, or even respond

It seemed He just blessed me from so far beyond

I sat on the bed just trying to understand

While I was asleep, I was visited by the man

We all seem to want so much from this world

Whether it is given as a gift, or has the value of a pearl

Yet God blesses everyone with what He feels is fit

But very few understand, it's His plan we don't get

So He gives us troubles, so He gives us pain

Because He wants our praise, whether it's through sunshine or rain

Yet the one thing He never did was teach the world fear

His son said trust Him, it's my father's voice you will hear

Because we all go through trials, as we take our walk

Yet if we just become grateful, God's spirit will talk

So before you lie down, look up and give our Lord praise

Be thankful He's been beside you for all of your days

Ronnie Fletcher

2/10/14

## A New Season

Now people, this message is one that might scare you

It had to be powerful, for those who live life without a clue

Do you think things happen to you for no reason?

Pay attention to life or you could miss your new season

Do things take place around you, and you can't explain why?

Moments in your life that make you think you would die

Do you feel everything around you is simply going wrong?

Pull it together; you're being tested to see if you belong

Well, today's message may be hard, but let us begin

While you are feeling sorry for yourself, nothing just happens

People will come into your path and act as a friend

Yet if they leave you, it may feel like the end

Situations may arise that may seem like all hell is breaking loose

Or you might come into happiness like a golden goose

You might meet someone who normally wouldn't catch your eye

Yet as you sit and talk, you feel close and don't know why

The day might come when you meet someone without a thing

Yet when you see them, it's your smile that they bring

All your life, you might cross people, but none who could win

It's your heart that draws a smile as feelings begin

Our steps are ordered by God and everything happens for a reason

So pick up your sadness, you're coming into a new season

Ronnie Fletcher

2/13/14

## God is Love

Today we learned the true meaning of love

It's not about lust it's about our Lord from above

Today was a day that life took a turn toward understanding

Are you ready to learn what God is commanding?

Today was a day that we had to turn back the years

Are you ready to adjust all of your troubles and fears?

Since we became adults, since the beginning of time

We always ignored the signs that pointed toward a crime

Now today's message was simple, if you wanted to learn

Yet most would rather be stubborn, not willing to turn

The 10 commandments were God's only laws for the world

They were meant to be followed by every boy and girl

Yet Jesus knew people could never follow them all

So Jesus only asked that you follow two, a request not so tall

The first one was to love God like you love yourself

Now this would mean you love unconditionally and keep in good health

The second one was to love thy neighbor like you love yourself

This would make the other commandments followed, just like wealth

Because when you realize God always commanded us to love

This was the message that was always sent from above

You won't hurt anyone that you truly love like yourself

That's because with God, you will find your own true wealth

Ronnie Fletcher

2/17/14

## It is the Lord

John 21:7

Now people this message is one to remember

It was delivered with energy to every single member

While the bishop spoke, there was a rumble among us

The congregation listened closely, but no one put up a fuss

The bishop yelled, how do you think you've obtained what you cannot afford?

This wasn't a stroke of luck, it was our Lord

When your enemies came to tear you down, but they lost the fight

It was the Lord who stepped in and commanded not tonight

When you had those problems that you knew had no chance

It was the Lord's hand who asked you for this dance

Don't get it twisted, don't you lose your sight

It is the Lord's will that gives you blessings every night

While you continue to receive things and don't understand why

It is the Lord's will that watches you from the sky

So when non-believers or strangers ask you how

It is the Lord's will, and not a cash cow

So when people admire what you have or what you've done

Respond "It is the Lord" my holy one

Ronnie Fletcher

2/19/14

## My Testimony

My sick young brother had called out to me

As I entered the hospital, I was escorted by Thee

My brother was saved from his saddened past

He spoke of a church, his soul it had grasped

My brother spoke of the members' open hearts

He said my brother go visit, seek a fresh start

You could see my brother had spoken while in pain

I promised to visit, as his tears brought the rain

Palm Sunday it was, I showed up with doubt

As I entered His house, people began to shout

They grabbed my hands, formed a circle in praise

A spirit of hope sent me in a daze

I watched as they prayed for my young sick brother

The Lord was within them as they prayed to no other

I started to sweat as they prayed for my fears

They continued to pray as my eyes filled with tears

The moment had passed, I sat down to give praise

Filled with emotion, never in my days

Another preacher came and spoke of Thee

She commanded the crowd to change I to We

All who are without a blessing of a job

Raise your hand whether you are Susan or Bob

Those who are blessed to still be employed

Place your hand on them, as His spirit is deployed

I turned to a lady who stood in the crowd

Placed my hand on her shoulder as she cried aloud

Her body trembled while she prayed on this day

Scared by her reaction, my heart filled today

Touched by the Lord, I vowed to return

The Lord smiled at me, for I have much to learn.

Fletch

March 2009

115